# SPORTS
# AND
# SOCIAL VALUES

**ROBERT L. SIMON**
*Hamilton College*

PRENTICE-HALL, INC., Englewood Cliffs, New Jersey 07632

**Library of Congress Cataloging in Publication Data**

Simon, Robert L., 1941–
    Sports and social values

    Includes bibliographical references and index.
1. Sports—Social aspects.  2. Sports—Social
aspects—United States.  I. Title.
GV706.5.S56  1985        306'.483'0973        84-16024
ISBN 0-13-837881-9

Editorial/production supervision and
  interior design: Kate Kelly
Cover design: Photo Plus Art
Manufacturing buyer: Harry P. Baisley

©1985 by Prentice-Hall, Inc., Englewood Cliffs, New Jersey 07632

Printed in the United States of America

10  9  8  7  6  5  4  3  2  1

ISBN 0-13-837881-9        01

Prentice-Hall International Inc., *London*
Prentice-Hall of Australia Pty. Limited, *Sydney*
Editora Prentice-Hall do Brasil, Ltda., *Rio de Janeiro*
Prentice-Hall Canada Inc., *Toronto*
Prentice-Hall of India Private Limited, *New Delhi*
Prentice-Hall of Japan, Inc., *Tokyo*
Prentice-Hall of Southeast Asia Pte, Ltd., *Singapore*
Whitehall Books Limited, *Wellington, New Zealand*

To my parents, who perhaps now finally will believe that the many hours I spent playing ball instead of doing homework really were "field research" after all.

# CONTENTS

# PREFACE

Sports play a significant role in the lives of millions of people throughout the world. While many men and women participate actively in sports, still more are spectators, fans, critics, and occasional participants. Indeed, it is quite common for the same individual to be a participant on one occasion and a spectator on another. Those who are uninvolved in sports or bored by them may be critical of athletics or of sports enthusiasts, whose behavior must sometimes seem impossible to understand.

Moreover, as a significant form of social activity, sports affect the educational system, the economy, and the values of citizens. While sociologists, psychologists, and physicians have shown increasing interest in sport as a distinct human activity, philosophers have lagged behind their colleagues in applying their own tools of analysis to sport.

Such attention is needed, however, for sports raise many serious conceptual and ethical questions. Should sport be accorded the importance it is assigned in our society? Is there too much emphasis on winning and competition? Are college sports getting out of hand? Are some sports, such as boxing or football, too violent? What are the requirements of sex equality in sports? Should we aim more for excellence in competition for the few or for greater participation in sport by the many? *Sports and Social Values* examines such questions and evaluates the principles thoughtful persons might appeal to when attempting to formulate answers.

Not only are questions in the philosophy of sport important in their own right, an examination of philosophical issues in sport can be of unusual pedagogical value. Most students come to philosophy courses with an awareness of and often deep interest in sports. That initial interest can be used as a launching pad to introduce beginners to philosophical analysis. Moreover, since many readers will participate in and observe sporting events, they may have to deal personally with the issues to be examined. A philosophical treatment of those issues may help them to formulate, clarify, and examine their own views.

Perhaps most important, issues in the philosophy of sport are of great intrinsic interest and are well worth our attention. Philosophical questions force us to stretch our analytical powers to the fullest and to question basic presuppositions. Those that arise in the philosophical examination of sport, like any others, require us to formulate, test, and evaluate fundamental principles of morality and engage in rigorous critical inquiry.

*Sports and Social Values* raises philosophical and ethical questions about sports in a manner accessible to introductory students and the general public, while at the same time illustrating how philosophical analysis can clarify and help resolve the difficult moral and conceptual issues at stake.


## ACKNOWLEDGMENTS

*Sports and Social Values* would never have been written had it not been for the challenges to my own views of sports put forth by friends, colleagues, and students. While all of my intellectual debts cannot be sorted out and acknowledged here, I would in particular like to thank Ray O'Connell of Prentice-Hall for suggesting the idea of such a book to me and my editor, Doris Michaels, for her encouragement, advice, and enthusiasm for the project. Thanks are also due to outside readers for Prentice-Hall for their reactions, to which I hope I have been able to do some justice.

A number of colleagues and friends have read and commented on sections of the book and made many helpful suggestions for its improvement. Particular thanks are due to the administration, staff, and many of the Fellows of the National Humanities Center during the 1981–1982 academic year for their enthusiasm for the project and willingness to discuss ethical issues in sport with me, although all of us were engaged in other projects at the time. Colleagues at Hamilton College, including Russell Blackwood, David Gray, David Paris, Betty Ring, and Rick Werner made many suggestions for improvement or raised fundamental questions about my views on sport. They, of course, are not responsible for what I say here or for the many comments of theirs which I no doubt foolishly rejected.

I would also like to thank my wife, Joy, not only for her critical help with the manuscript, but also for putting up with an abnormal number of fits of abstraction ("Earth calling Bob" became one of the phrases used most often at our dinner table conversations) while this book was being written. Sports has been one of the major activities my family and I have shared so I hope they enjoy reading the finished product as much as I did writing it.

Finally, without the participants in sport who demonstrate the kind of quest for excellence discussed in Chapter Two, much of the subject matter of philosophy of sport would be empty abstraction. In particular, my family and I wish to thank past and present staff and players in the Hamilton College men's and women's basketball program for not only getting me away from the typewriter but for making the harsh upstate New York winter one of the most exciting and pleasurable times of year.

# CHAPTER ONE
# INTRODUCTION
# TO THE PHILOSOPHY
# OF SPORT

I would like to think that this book began on an unfortunately not atypical cold and rainy late October day in upstate New York. I had been discussing some of my generally unsuccessful competitive efforts in local golf tournaments with colleagues in the Philosophy Department and let drop what I thought was an innocuous remark to the effect that while winning isn't everything, it sure beats losing. Much to my surprise my colleagues objected vehemently, asserting that winning means nothing. On their view, all that matters is playing well. I soon found myself backed into a corner by this hitherto unthreatening but now fully aroused assortment of philosophers. Fortunately, at just the right moment, another colleague entered the office. Struck by the vehemence of the argument, although he had no idea what it was about, he looked at my opponents and remarked, "You guys sure are trying to win this argument."

This incident illustrates two assumptions that underlie the philosophy of sports. First, issues exist in sports which are not simply empirical ones to be examined by such disciplines as psychology or sociology. Psychology and sociology can tell us whether people think winning is important and can help explain why people participate in competitive sports. But these disciplines cannot tell us if winning really *is* important or whether athletes should have winning as their primary goal. Second, the incident showed that logic could be applied to issues in the philosophy of sport. Thus, at least on the surface, it appeared that my colleagues were in the logically embarrassing position of trying hard to win an argument to the effect that winning is unimportant.

We will return to the issue of the importance of winning in Chapter Two. For now, however, let us consider further what philosophy might contribute to the study of sports.

## SPORTS, PHILOSOPHY, AND MORAL VALUES

### Sports and Human Life

Sports play a major if often unappreciated role in the lives of Americans. Most of us are exposed to them as children. As a result of our childhood experiences, many of us become participants or fans for life, while many others are appalled by their experiences and avoid sports like the plague. They may have been embarrassed by failures in front of peers or humiliated by an insensitive physical education instructor. Some may just find sports boring.

Most of us, however, retain some affiliation with sports for life, even if only as spectators. Indeed, the extent of American involvement with sports is amazing. According to the recent Miller Lite Report on American Attitudes toward sports, one of the most extensive and systematic studies done in this area, 96.3 percent of the American population plays or watches or reads articles about sport with some frequency or identifies with particular teams or players.[1] Moreover, nearly 70 percent follow sports every day while 42 percent participate on a daily basis.[2]

Although intensity of involvement cannot always be measured as effectively as extent of involvement, there is little doubt that sports are a meaningful element of our lives. Indeed, the time and effort athletes and fans devote to sport at all levels suggest they find involvement in sports one of the most significant and valuable experiences they enjoy.

Moreover, the situation is not unique to the United States. Intense interest in sports is a common phenomenon globally. Whether it is ice hockey in the U.S.S.R. or soccer in Europe, South America, and Africa, intense interest in sports is found worldwide. Sport was valued by the ancient Greeks, by the Romans, and by the American Indians. Indeed, it is arguable that sports are an important element of virtually every known culture, present and past.

As a result, it is no wonder that sports are increasingly attracting the attention of scholars. Sociologists of sport study its place in society. Psychologists of sport study the relationships of sports and individual behavior and sometimes even advise major teams or athletes on how to improve their performance through the application of psychology. Best selling popular books, such as *The Inner Game of Tennis,* apply more scholarly, theoretical studies to the performances of the average participant.

What does philosophy have to contribute to this inquiry into sports? It is evident to even a casual observer of our society that sports in America, particularly organized sports, are undergoing intense moral examination. Intercollegiate sports are afflicted by recruiting scandals, which involve submission of false transcripts, under-the-table payments to college athletes, and cheating on entrance examinations. As a result, many question whether any form of big-time sports belongs on a college or university campus. At the professional level, observers wonder whether the effects of big money and television exposure have corrupted the essense of sporting competition.[3] When athletes, who used to be revered as heroes, are arrested for the use of cocaine, and when players are often regarded as spoiled and overpaid, can the best of athletic competition still be preserved? What does social justice require with respect to the increasing participation of women in sport? What constitutes sex discrimination in sport and what rules regarding it should be adopted and applied?

These and similar questions raise basic issues about the kinds of moral values involved in sports. Does too much emphasis on winning corrupt children's sports and lead to the abuses on the college level? Does the lavish adulation we devote to good athletes, often at the expense of the masses of participants, result in the exploitation of athletes by the colleges and what might be regarded as the spoiled and insensitive behavior of some professional players toward the general public? Questions such as these are not about what people do think or even about how they think. They are about what people *ought* to think. They require the identification and application of *defensible standards of evaluation* to sport. The formulation and criticism of such standards, as well as their application to concrete issues, is a major part of the business of philosophy of sport.

### Philosophy of Sports

Misconceptions about the nature of philosophy are widespread. According to one story, a philosopher on a domestic airline flight was asked by his seatmate what he did for a living. He replied, perhaps foolishly, "I'm a philosopher."[4] His companion, apparently stupified by the reply, was silent for several minutes. Finally, he turned to the philosopher and remarked, "Oh, and what are some of your sayings?"

The image of the philosopher as the author of wise sayings can perhaps be forgiven, since the word "philosophy" has its roots in the Greek expression for "love of wisdom." However, wisdom is not necessarily encapsuled in brief sayings which we might memorize before breakfast. The famous ancient Greek philosopher, Socrates, provides a different model of philosophic inquiry.

Socrates, who lived in the fifth century B.C., did not leave a body of written work behind him, but we know a good deal about his life from the writings of his most famous pupil, Plato, and other sources. As a young man, Socrates, who was seeking a mentor from whom to learn, set out to find the wisest man in Greece. He decided to ask an important religious figure, the Oracle at Delphi, the identity of the man in question. Much to Socrates' surprise, the Oracle informed him that he, Socrates, was the wisest man in Greece. "How can that be?" Socrates must have wondered, since it was precisely because he was ignorant that he was looking for a wise teacher with whom he could study.

However, looking at the Oracle's reply in light of Plato's presentation of Socrates in his early dialogues, we can discern what the Oracle might have meant. In such dialogues as the *Euthyphro,* Socrates is pictured as questioning various important figures on such topics as the nature of piety or the essense of knowledge. Those questioned purport to be experts in the subject at hand, but their expertise is dissolved under the fire of Socratic logical analysis. They don't know what they claim to know; indeed the so-called experts seem to thoughtlessly accept views which they had never exposed to critical examination.

Perhaps what the Oracle had in mind, then, in calling Socrates the wisest man in Greece, was to suggest that Socrates alone was willing to expose his beliefs and principles to critical examination. He did not claim to know what he in fact did not know but was willing to learn. He was not willing to take popular opinion for granted but wished to question it.

This suggests that the role of philosophy might be to examine our beliefs, clarify the principles on which they rest, and subject them to critical examination. Although the relationship between philosophy and science is controversial, it is probably safe to say that philosophy differs from science at least in the generality of its examination and in the nature of the issues it deals with. Philosophy has a more general scope of inquiry than science, for example, in that it can ask questions *about* science from the outside. For example, philosophers may question whether or not scientific inquiry is the only way of gaining knowledge or whether there might also be such other sources of knowledge as individual intuition or religious revelation. Similarly, many of the questions philosophers ask do not seem answerable by scientific methods. "Is winning important in sports?" is a question about values, which at least on the surface, seems different from the kind of factual, empirical, or explanatory questions which scientists ask. Or if it is really a scientific question, despite appearances, then we will need philosophical argument to establish its true nature.

If we adopt such a broad view of philosophy, the task of philosophy of sport would be to clarify, systematize, and evaluate the principles we believe should govern the world of sport. This might involve conceptual inquiry into the meaning of such terms as "sport" and "game," aesthetic inquiry into the nature of excellence in athletics, ethical evaluation of general principles such as "Winning should be the only concern of the serious athlete," and application of ethical analysis to concrete controversies, such as disagreement over whether athletes should be permitted to take allegedly performance enhancing drugs such as steroids.

This book will be concerned primarily with the ethical evaluation of principles which many people apply to sports and application of the analysis to specific issues. Its major focus will be on the nature of principles and values which *should* apply in the realm of sports. Thus, its concern is predominantly *normative* rather than *descriptive*. Many individuals never think of sports in moral terms. They see sports as a mere instrument for attaining fame and fortune, or as play, an activity we engage in for fun and recreation but not as one which raises serious moral issues. But as we will see, important moral issues which require serious examination do arise in sport.

But is rational argument over ethical issues even possible? Are moral views just matters of opinion? After all, who is to say what is correct or incorrect? Can moral principles even be correct or incorrect or are they mere expressions of personal feelings?

## ETHICS AND MORAL REASONING

The sceptical questions posed above involve complex issues which require far more extensive treatment than can be given here. However, some useful introductory distinctions can be made. After all, if reasoned ethical discourse is impossible, rational inquiry into the moral basis of sports would be pointless. In this section, some widely cited reasons for doubting whether reasoned inquiry into moral issues is possible will be examined and an account will be provided of some proposed tools of moral reasoning.

### Relativism

It is widely believed that moral judgments made within one cultural tradition are contradicted by moral judgments made within other cultural traditions. Moral judgments also conflict within cultures, frequently along religious, ethnic and socioeconomic lines. For example, people from different religious groups may differ along religious lines on the morality of abortion. At another level, secular culture in the West tends to cast a permissive eye toward sexual contact between unmarried but consenting adults, but in other times and places such contacts have been and are regarded as highly immoral.

What has been asserted so far is a descriptive claim about how the world is. According to *descriptive relativism*, moral judgments are relative to the culture, religion, socioeconomic circumstances, or background of the observer. That is, the moral judgments people make differ, and often conflict, because of the different backgrounds of the evaluators.

What does this have to do with rational inquiry in ethics? The connection is this: It can be argued that if descriptive relativism is true, moral judgments are only reflections of one's cultural, social, economic, or religious background. People from different backgrounds cannot be expected to agree on moral issues since there is nothing to agree about. Moral views are just the prejudices we absorbed as children. Perhaps they were presented to us as self-evident truths. In reality, they are only the blinders of our particular culture or group.

Stated more formally, the argument looks like this.

1.  People from different cultural, religious, and socioeconomic backgrounds make conflicting moral judgments.
2.  Therefore, there is no correct resolution of their disagreement; each group is bound only by its own morality.
3.  Therefore, rational inquiry designed to rationally resolve such disagreement is pointless.

Premise (1) is the thesis of *descriptive relativism*. It is used to support the principle of *ethical relativism* stated in (2). (1) is a factual claim about the judgments people make while (2) denies that a rational resolution of moral disagreements of the kind in question is even possible. Finally, (3) maintains that since a rational resolution of moral disagreements is impossible, a rational inquiry designed to find such a solution has no point to begin with.

### A Critique of Relativism

Fortunately for the task of this book, the argument from (1) to (2) and (3) is very weak. To see this, consider what conditions an argument must satisfy to be acceptable. Surely, if we are to accept the conclusion of an argument on the basis of the premises, two minimal conditions must be satisfied. First, the premises must be true. Surely, false premises do not provide grounds for the truth of a conclusion. Second, the premises must be logically relevant to supporting the conclusion. Thus, we would not accept the conclusion, "The major goal of participation in sport is to win" on the basis of the premise "Washington D.C. is the capital of the United States" since the latter has absolutely nothing to do with the former.

The relativistic argument can be criticized as failing to satisfy each of these conditions; the truth condition and the logical relevance condition.

Consider premise (1), which states that people from different groups make conflicting moral judgments. If this means that they *sometimes* make conflicting moral judgments, it surely is true. But that leaves open the possibility that they sometimes, even usually, agree in moral judgments. The areas of agreement might constitute the basis of cross-cultural *universal* values, which some social scientists and sociobiologists have claimed to detect. For example, people from a wide variety of ethnic, cultural, socioeconomic, and religious backgrounds can be expected to condemn incest, the random torture and killing of a member of their community for momentary enjoyment, or the smearing of one's children with jelly and subsequent throwing of them to the army ants for Saturday night entertainment. There are grounds, then, for doubting the truth of (1) if it is meant to state that differences in group background always, or even usually, lead to moral disagreement in judgment.

However, even if we ignore this point, we should not conclude that disagreement in *moral judgment* necessarily reflects disagreement in *moral principle*. Even if different cultures, religions, ethnic groups, or social classes differ radically in their judgments on particular cases, such disagreement may rest on a broader basis of moral agreement in principle.

For instance, consider a dispute between a football coach and his assistant before the big game. The head coach believes his offense should rely on passing to exploit a weakness in the opponent's secondary pass defense. The assistant believes the offense should rely on a running game because of a weakness in the opponent's line play. In this case, both coaches may accept the same strategic principle—exploit your opponent's major weakness—but apply the principle differently since each believes their opponent has a different weakness.

A parallel situation is possible in ethics. Suppose Culture A believes old people should be left out to die when they can no longer contribute to the group but Culture B disagrees. Clearly, there is a disagreement in judgment about how old people should be treated. But does this reflect an underlying disagreement in principle? Not necessarily.

For one thing, the circumstances of each culture might differ. Culture A might be on the verge of extinction. Its roving nomadic groups cannot afford to support those who can't contribute. If the old are not left out to die, even more deaths will result in the long run. Culture B may be affluent and face no such difficulty. Thus, both cultures might accept the same moral principle—do what promotes the most good for the most people—but the principle itself might apply differently in different circumstances. Once again, step (1), even if true, does not rule out the existence of universally accepted values on the level of moral principle.

Perhaps the greatest weakness of the relativist argument is that it fails the test of logical relevance. Premise (1), even if true, does not provide significant support for (2), nor does (2) lead logically to (3). Even if there are no universally accepted ethical values—if every judgment or principle accepted by one culture is rejected by another—this does not prove that rational resolution of moral disputes is impossible. The fact that cultures, or even individual people, disagree does not show there are no correct answers.

One might as well argue that because some cultures believe the earth is flat, or some deny that bacteria (rather than gremlins) cause infections, there is no correct answer to whether or not the earth is round or whether or not infection is caused by germs. The mere existence of a disagreement does not prove, or even suggest, that there is no correct answer to the question being disputed, let alone that different fundamental moral or scientific principles apply to different groups.[5]

Of course, it doesn't necessarily follow that there *is* a correct solution to ethical disputes. All that has been claimed so far is that cultures, religions, or social classes can make conflicting moral judgments, and one or more parties to the conflict can be *wrong* or mistaken in their moral views.

Finally, even if there is no one correct answer to important ethical disputes—or if such an answer cannot be discovered by human investigators—it does not follow that rational inquiry in ethics is pointless. Step (2) of the relativist's argument does not entail step (3). Even if rational inquiry in ethics does not yield correct answers in the sense that mathematics or science is said to, it may free us from our prejudices, lead us to discard beliefs based on false factual information and help us to better understand the views of others. As we will see, moral inquiry, even if it does not yield truth, may be able to distinguish moral views that are reasonable from those that are not and separate more warranted from less warranted opinions and principles.

Therefore, the mere "fact" of ethical disagreement between cultures, religions, or socioeconomic classes should not deter us from engaging in moral inquiry. Only by attempting to rationally resolve moral disputes can we test our own moral views and those of others by subjecting them to critical evaluation. Perhaps moral disputes are empty and cannot be resolved since they involve only conflicts of opinion. To *assume* that just because people disagree there are no right answers is itself to hold on to a blind prejudice which cannot withstand rational scrutiny and criticism.

### If It Feels Good, It Must Be Right

Someone unpersuaded by our critique of relativism might retort: "Perhaps you have shown that mere disagreement by itself doesn't show that rational resolution of moral disagreement is impossible. But what does establish such a conclusion is the nature of ethical judgments themselves. They are just expressions of the feelings and emotions of the speaker. Since feelings and emotions can't be true or false, or warranted or unwarranted, neither can moral judgments."

On this view, moral judgments are just expressions of emotion. According to this analysis, someone who claims that use of anabolic steroids by Olympic athletes is wrong is simply expressing a feeling. Moral judgments turn out to be sophisticated ways of saying "Great!" or "Ychhh!" Since neither the former nor latter is true or false, neither are the more sophisticated moral judgments, which appear to make claims but really say no more than the emotional ejaculations for which they substitute.

In its sophisticated philosophical form, this theory is known as *emotivism*.[6] Like the once popular California bumper sticker, "If it feels good, it must be right," emotivism identifies morality with feelings, but while the sticker makes feeling the test of rightness, emotivism rejects the idea of a test and identifies talk of rightness with *expression* of feeling. While an extensive examination of emotivism is beyond the scope of our inquiry, enough can be said to call into question any crude or simple identification of moral judgments with expressions of emotion or claims about our feelings.[7]

To begin with, moral judgments are not the only kind of linguistic entities that express emotion or feeling. The golfer who says, "It's raining" may be expressing deep disgust *but also* saying something true, which is subject to testing and investigation. Similarly, even if moral judgments sometimes do express emotions or feelings, they might also make claims which are true or false, warranted or unwarranted, or rational or irrational. One does not preclude the other.

Perhaps more to the point, if morality amounted to nothing but the expression of feelings and emotions—if it had no rational, cognitive, or intellectual content—it should not be possible to morally evaluate our feelings and emotions. But this is precisely what we are able to do. Consider, for example, someone brought up in a cultural context where it is believed that women must never speak up or contradict men in public. Our subject leaves her home and moves to a large sophisticated urban center. There she finds a different moral code in force and is taught at the university that the customs of her people reflect ancient beliefs about sex differences which function as a device to keep women in their place and assign power to men. While she intellectually understands such an analysis, she continues to experience revulsion whenever she sees a woman contradict a man in public. But while she feels disgust at such a sight, she questions her feelings: "I feel this is morally outrageous and disgusting, but is it really morally outrageous and disgusting?"

If her moral views were nothing but feelings and emotions, it would make no sense for her to morally question them. That she, and the rest of us, can consider whether our feelings and emotions really are morally appropriate suggests that there is a higher court of moral appeal than the feelings and emotions themselves. Contrary to slogans on bumper stickers, something may feel good, but it is not necessarily morally right. Moreover, in saying something is wrong, we are not necessarily expressing only an emotional reaction.

## Who Is To Say?

Sometimes during a heated moral argument, someone—often the person losing the debate—will interject, "But who is to say who is right?" Although this remark often functions as a conversation stopper, there is no reason why it should automatically call serious moral reflection to a halt.

If "Who is to say?" is put forth as a request for good reasons, it often is appropriate. Thus, if one is arguing about whether or not boxing is inherently immoral because it is so violent, and one's opponent just keeps asserting "Boxing is horrible and disgusting and evil," then one may very well ask, "Who is to say?"

But if one asks "Who is to say?" as a means of blocking a search for reasons, the move is not legitimate. Thus, if the opponent of boxing argues that boxing is wrong because it involves inflicting pain on another human and that the infliction of pain is wrong, one must come up with a counter-argument in order to avoid the conclusion. As a response to argument, the rejoinder "Who is to say?" functions more as a rhetorical escape valve for avoiding defeat than as a genuine contribution to the debate. The obvious answer to "Who is to say?" is that the individual with the best reasons has the best grounds for saying.

## Moral Reasoning

But how are we to distinguish good from bad moral reasoning? Philosophers and ethicists have not agreed on any one theory of moral reasoning. Indeed, it is doubtful if one can evaluate moral arguments with the kind of precision and rigor that might be employed in elementary arithmetic. That does not mean, however, that there are no acceptable standards that can be used to distinguish well-thought-out and well-supported moral positions from illogical or badly supported ones. All reasoning is not of the form of mathematical proof. As Aristotle suggested, we should "look for precision in each class of things just so far as the nature of the subject admits; it is evidently equally foolish to accept probable reasoning from a mathematician and to demand from a rhetorician scientific proofs."[8]

This does not mean ethical reasoning must be imprecise or sloppy, but that it may well be more like the making of a case by a skilled judicial scholar than a strict proof. In evaluating ethical issues, the following criteria of good moral reasoning may prove helpful.

First, moral reasoning must be *impartial*. In evaluating a moral issue, we are not asking, "What's in it for me?" Rather, our goal is to see what position is supported by the best reasons impartially considered. Moral deliberation, in other words, is deliberation from a moral perspective, not that of self-interest. Thus, we cannot justify the claim "The use of steroids of Olympic athletes is morally acceptable" simply by claiming "The use of steroids will help me win a gold medal." The latter claim may show that the use of steroids is in the speaker's interest. It does nothing to show that personal interest is the only morally relevant factor.

R. M. Hare, distinguished professor of philosophy at Oxford University, has suggested that impartial moral reasoning, at its most sophisticated, requires that we imagine ourselves in the place of all others affected by the action or policy being evaluated, giving no special weight to any one person's perspective.[9] John Rawls of Harvard, author of the important book, *A Theory of Justice,* has suggested that in thinking of social justice, we must reason as if were behind a veil of ignorance which obscures from us knowledge of our personal characteristics or social circumstances.[10] Regardless of similarities or dissimilarities between these two conceptions of impartiality in ethics, each prevents us from assigning special weight to our own circumstances or interest. Yet each may have practical application. It would seem irrational, for example, to assign inferior status to any racial groups if we had to consider the result from the position of all affected, as Hare requires, or if were in ignorance of which racial group we belong to, as Rawls suggests.

If we are to reason morally, we must reason from an impartial perspective. In addition, the positions we advance from that perspective must be systematically *consistent.* That is, we cannot take a position on one issue which contradicts our position on another. Since one contradicts the other, both cannot be true or acceptable. For example, if one holds both that it is impermissible for weight lifters to take steroids for their own benefit and that it is permissible for players on the hometown football team to take steroids, one has a serious intellectual problem. The problem can be avoided either by showing that the two situations are dissimilar, so that no contradiction arises, or by abandoning one of the positions.

Thirdly, one's position must account for our reflective judgment on clear moral examples. For example, any moral position which implied there was nothing wrong with smearing babies with jelly and throwing them to the army ants would be suspect for that very reason.

We must be sure, of course, that our reaction to specific cases is critical and reflective. It is all too easy to be influenced by cultural, social, and even biologically based presuppositions which cloud our appreciation of what is at stake. However, our reflective reaction to actual and hypothetical examples seems to be a useful guide to moral evaluation. Without consideration of cases, our principles would be empty abstractions. We would have no appreciation of their significance in action for human life.

It also would seem that the more an ethical position survives criticism and counterexample, the more confidence we are entitled to place in it. Just as we should want to expose our scientific theories to experimental test, so we should want to test our moral positions by exposing them to the criticism of others. It may make us feel good to cling to our moral views by never exposing them to opposing viewpoints. But the price we pay for such a policy is that we close ourselves off from discovering any errors we might be making and from opportunities for confirming our views through refutation of objections. Just as a scientific theory gains in credibility through surviving tests, so may a moral view gain credibility by continually surviving objections in the crucible of moral debate.

Nothing said so far implies that only one moral viewpoint, perspective, or theory will survive moral criticism. Possibly all who go through a process of moral inquiry guided by the sorts of criteria we have considered will tend to agree on one position. It is also possible that a kind of moral pluralism will flourish. It is doubtful, however, that rigorous moral investigators will rate *all* approaches as equally warranted. Some will be rejected as inconsistent, biased, or vulnerable to counterexample. Thus, while there is no guarantee that our criteria of moral reasoning are the only ones, or that they will inevitably support one view over all others, they at least provide guidance in the attempt to derive a rationally defensible position on moral issues. By applying them, we employ reason in ethics.

Let us turn, then, to the discussion of moral issues in sports. We will begin with an examination of a fundamental issue: the degree of importance that should be assigned to competition and winning in sports.

## NOTES

[1]Reported by George Vecsey, "A Nation of Sports Fans," *The New York Times,* March 16, 1983, p. B11.

[2]Ibid.

[3]David Halberstam, *The Breaks of the Game* (New York: Alfred A. Knopf, 1981) is a fascinating book which considers the ill effects of big salaries on a championship professional basketball team.

[4]I owe this story to Professor Ed Pincoffs, who assures me it is true.

[5]At this point, there may be a temptation to reply that of course disagreement in mathematics or science doesn't show the lack of a correct answer, but *ethics is different.* However, the whole point of the relativistic argument is to *establish* that ethics is different. It can't use in the premises the very point it is trying to establish in the conclusion without begging the question.

[6]Probably the most sophisticated philosophical account and defense of emotivism is found in C. L. Stevenson's *Ethics and Language* (New Haven: Yale University Press, 1945).

[7]For a more extended critique of emotivism, see Roger N. Hancock, *Twentieth Century Ethics* (New York: Columbia University Press, 1974), Chapter Four.

[8]Aristotle, *Nicomachean Ethics*, Bk. I., Chap 2, 25, translated by W. D. Ross, in Richard McKeon, ed. *The Basic Works of Aristotle* (New York: Random House, 1941), p. 936.

[9]See particularly R. M. Hare, *Freedom and Reason* (New York: Oxford University Press, 1965).

[10]John Rawls, *A Theory of Justice* (Cambridge: Harvard University Press, 1971).

# CHAPTER TWO
# THE ETHICS
# OF COMPETITION

"Winning is not the most important thing: it's the only thing." This widely cited claim, often attributed (perhaps falsely) to the late Vince Lombardi, raises a host of issues that are central to the moral evaluation of sport.[1] What importance should be assigned to winning in athletic competition? Consider sportswriter Grantland Rice's declaration that "When the Great Scorer comes to mark against your name, He writes not that you won or lost but how you played the Game," as well as the rejoinder by coach Forest Evashevski that one might as well say of a surgeon that it matters not whether his patient lives or dies but only how he makes the cut.[2]

Questions about the importance of winning are closely tied to, but not identical with, questions about the value of competition. Should we be concerned primarily with winning or with competing well? We will begin our inquiry by considering the nature and value of competition in sports and athletics. The results can then be applied to an investigation of the importance of winning.

## COMPETITION IN SPORTS

At first glance, competition seems almost built into the very nature of sport. We speak of sporting events as contests or competitions, describe athletes as good or bad competitors, and refer to those on other teams as opponents.

However, the connection between sport and competition is far looser than such an initial reaction might suggest. Fishing and skiing are sports but neither necessarily involves competition. Indeed, virtually any sport can be played noncompetitively. Men and women may participate to get away from work, to exercise, because they enjoy physical activity, to make friends and meet new people, or to enjoy fresh air. Another goal of participants might be improvement. Such players, often misleadingly described as "competing with themselves," aim not at defeating opponents but at improving their own personal performance. Still others may have the purely aesthetic goal of making the movements of their sport with skill and grace. For example, basketball players may value outstanding moves rather than defeat of opponents. A leading amateur golfer, after years of hard practice, describes her aim as "to make a swing that you know is as close to perfection as you can get. And you say, 'Boy, look at what I did.' That's all it is."[3]

None of these goals necessarily exclude competitiveness or a desire to win. One can value exercise, try to improve, appreciate skilled moves, *and* compete. What must be added to clear examples of noncompetitive sport, however, in order to derive a clear case of competition in sport?

If we are to evaluate competition in the context of sports or athletics, we first must be able to identify it and distinguish it from noncompetitive sport.[4] Are there any specific elements that distinguish competitive from noncompetitive participation in sports?

It is possible that no common features are present in all sports. Perhaps there is at most a family resemblance.[5] Be that as it may, there do seem to be elements that are central to *clear* or *paradigm cases* of competition in sports. By focusing on such clear cases, we can insure that central aspects of competition are being dealt with and leave borderline or puzzling instances for case-by-case analysis.

What seems missing from participation in sport as a means to improvement, exercise, and aesthetic appreciation is the goal of defeating an opponent. In clear cases at least, competition seems to be a form of zero-sum game. The aim, defeat of an opponent, cannot be obtained by all and attainment of the goal by one player (or team) precludes its attainment by others. Competition in sports and athletics, *at its most clear*, is participation with the goal of defeating opponents.[6]

Two further points require explanation. The clearest cases of athletic competition involve structured games such as baseball, field hockey, and football, all of which are governed by a series of rules which define or constitute the game in question. For example, the rules of basketball that stipulate what it is to score, to foul, and to travel are such *constitutive rules*. If players were unaware of such rules or made no effort to follow them, they would not be playing basketball (although minimal modifications might be accepted in informal play). Constitutive rules should be distinguished sharply from *rules of strategy* such as "Dribble only if there is no faster way of advancing the ball up the court." Rules of strategy are generalizations suggesting how to play the game well while constitutive rules determine what it is to play that particular game.

If individuals are competing in sport, their goal cannot be simply winning but must be to win within the framework set by the constitutive rules. Strictly speaking, since what counts as winning is defined by such rules, one cannot actually win by cheating, although of course a successful cheat may get others to believe he has won. Actually, since cheaters make moves not recognized by the constitutive rules of the sport, not only do they fail to prove themselves better players than other competitors, they may not even succeed in playing the game to begin with.[7]

Second, we should distinguish the conceptual claim that the *goal* of competition is victory from the psychological claim that the competitors' primary *motive* for participating is the desire to win. Players may participate solely because they relish the joy of competition. For them, it is the process of competition rather than the outcome which is important. If they were not trying to defeat their opponents, they would not be competing. But it doesn't follow that the main reason they have for competing is to win. Similarly, I may build model airplanes simply because I enjoy the activity of construction, but the activity I indulge in would not be that of building a model plane if my movements were not intended to result in the creation of a model plane.

Competition in sports and athletics paradigmatically is to be thought of as the attempt to secure victory within the appropriate constitutive rules defining the contest. How is competition in sports to be evaluated? Is it good or bad, fair or unfair, beneficial or harmful? Should it be tolerated, encouraged, or forbidden? It is to such questions that we now turn.

## THE CRITIQUE OF COMPETITION

Why is it necessary for us to morally evaluate competition in sports? Isn't it enough to say that participants and spectators alike enjoy such competition and voluntarily associate themselves with it? To critics of competition in sports, that is not enough. They argue that such competition is inherently immoral or, more cautiously, that it expresses and reinforces undesirable social values. Many persons, including some successful professional athletes, have criticized the overemphasis on winning which they believe the competitive attitude breeds, and have proposed a more relaxed attitude toward sports than that sanctioned by the competitive creed.

On the other hand, proponents of athletic competition have argued for its moral value. At their most extreme, they have held that the competitive spirit in sports is one foundation of the best elements of our national character. General Douglas MacArthur may have overstated the case when he maintained that participation in competitive sport "is a vital character builder" which "molds the youth of our country for their roles as custodians of the republic."[8] Overstated or not, the view he expressed is a widely shared one.

A moral assessment of competition in sport is necessary if we are to evaluate these different views. It is not enough to defend competition in sport on the grounds that it is fun, without hearing the arguments of the critics. After all, racist members of a dominant majority may enjoy terrorizing a racial minority but that doesn't make their behavior right. We need to rationally evaluate the arguments for and against the morality of competition in sport.

It will be useful to divide arguments about the moral justification of athletic competition into two kinds. The first kind is concerned with the good or bad effects of competitive practices, either on society generally or on the competitors themselves. The second focuses not on the effects of competition but on its intrinsic character. Does competition in sport, by its very nature, involve morally unacceptable features quite apart from its consequences?

An important moral defense of competition in sport is that it promotes good character. Let us deal first with this version of the consequentialist approach.

## The Consequences of Competition

One way of ethically evaluating competition in sport is to assess its consequences. Surely, whether a practice has good or bad consequences is relevant to our moral evaluation of it. However, while the strategy of evaluating competition by its consequences seems eminently sensible, carrying it out raises more difficulties than one might initially expect.

First of all, are we to evaluate the effects only on participants or are we to look at the consequences for everyone affected? The important ethical theory known as *utilitarianism* holds that a practice or activity is morally justified if and only if it has better consequences for all affected than any alternative. Otherwise, it is morally unjustified and we should adopt the practice or activity that does have the most favorable ratio of good to bad consequences. In practice, however, how are we to distinguish the effects of competition in sport upon the rest of society from the effect of competition in business, industry, science, or the academic world?

Perhaps we would do better by considering only the effects of competition in sport upon the competitors themselves. However, before we try to apply the utilitarian approach, we must decide what is to count as a good or bad consequence. For example, should we identify the good consequences with benefits actually experienced by competitors or with benefits they would experience *if* they were fully rational. Suppose that Jones is disgusted by her coach's emphasis on teamwork but would derive great benefit from it if she were more rational. Is the practice beneficial to Jones or not?

Even if we could answer this question, another arises. Just what practice are we evaluating? "Competition in sports" can encompass professional athletic contests, school yard basketball games, intercollegiate and interscholastic contests, and golf and tennis matches between friends. Principles that might apply in one kind of competition might need modification before being applied in others. Moreover, in each area, we need to distinguish competition as it is actually carried out from competition as it ought to be carried out. Thus, even if actual competitive practices often have bad consequences, we should not necessarily conclude that competition in sports in bad, harmful or indefensible. Perhaps actual competitive practices depart from an ideal of athletic competition; an ideal that would not have bad consequences if it were applied in action.

Any utilitarian evaluation of competition, then, will rest on a number of controversial presuppositions. In assessing the significance of such an evaluation we need to be clear just what presuppositions have been employed. For example, if a study shows that participation in competitive sport has little effect on character development, should we conclude that competition as such has no effect on character under all conditions? Or should we conclude that competition as practiced falls far short of a defensible ideal of competitive sport which would have beneficial effects on character if widely implemented?

While an exhaustive analysis of the effects of competition in sport is beyond the scope of this study, what can at least be suggested here is the need for sophistication and caution in assessing broad generalizations in this area.

Proponents of competitive sport, as we have seen, frequently claim that participation promotes such desirable traits as loyalty, discipline, commitment, a concern for excellence, and a "never-say-die" attitude. These views are expressed by well-known slogans, sometimes posted on the locker room wall, like "A quitter never wins, a winner never quits" and "When the going gets tough, the tough get going." Strongly stated generalizations, such as the assertion that "Athletics offer the greatest opportunity for character development of any activity" are common.[9] Unfortunately, even if we restrict ourselves to effects upon competitors under actual rather than ideal conditions, such claims are difficult to document. Thus, with regard to altruism, one recent study concludes that "Most athletes indicate low interest in receiving support and concern from others, low need to take care of others and low need for affiliation. Such a personality seems necessary to achieve victory over others."[10] More generally, the authors report

> We found no empirical support for the tradition that sport builds character. . . . It seems that the personality of the ideal athlete is not the result of any molding process, but comes out of the ruthless selection process that

occurs at all levels of sport. . . . Horatio Alger success—in sport or elsewhere—comes only to those who already are mentally fit, resilient and strong.[11]

Although no single study is decisive, this passage does suggest a number of important methodological conclusions. Even if participants in athletics do manifest desirable character traits to an unusual degree, it does not follow that participation in sport *caused* such traits to develop. Rather, it may have been prior possession of those traits that led to successful participation. *Correlation* should not be confused with *causation*.

However, by the same token, negative effects often attributed to competition need not be caused by competition itself. Thus, it has been suggested that "athletes whose sense of identity and self-worth is entirely linked to athletic achievement often experience an identity crisis when the athletic career has ended, and it becomes necessary to move on to something else."[12] However, this may be true generally of hard-driving individuals who face significant changes at the end of careers in other fields. Would anyone be surprised by the claim "executives whose sense of identity and self-worth is entirely linked to achievement in business often experience an identity crisis when their career has ended and it becomes necessary to move on to something else?" We need to distinguish causation from correlation in evaluating both the positive and negative aspects of competition in sport.

Moreover, empirical studies may fail to capture subtle indirect causal connections. Professor Harry Edwards, while acknowledging that competitive sports do not build character from scratch, suggests that participation in competitive sport may reinforce *and* encourage development of preexisting character traits.[13] Perhaps individuals with certain kinds of personalities tend to participate in competitive sport *and* have the relevant features of their character reinforced as a result. This suggests that it is not easy to show that participation in competitive sport either clearly does or clearly does not promote specific character traits in participants.

Even if competitive sport have less impact on character than many have claimed, they may play a major role in *expressing* and *illustrating* our values. This might be called the expressive function of sport.[14]

For example, athletic competition may illustrate the value of dedication and discipline by publicly manifesting the degree of excellence the cultivation of such traits can enable us to attain. Closely contested events may provide opportunities for exhibition of such personal virtues as courage, dedication, and loyalty. By welcoming challenges in sport, participants and supporters can affirm and exhibit the value of personal virtues and qualities.

In reply, critics might charge that athletic competition can also illustrate indefensible value commitments, such as the commitment to win at all costs. When applied to actual competitive practices, this response sometimes may have force. However, even if such criticism often does apply, we still need a model of what a defensible form of competition might be like, if only to serve as a basis for suggesting reforms of current practices.

What values should we want competition in sports to illustrate, express, and reinforce? To some critics, this question is misguided. On their view, competition is inherently immoral. Competitive values are the values of selfishness and inequality. If such views are correct, it would be a mistake to attempt to formulate a competitive ethic for application to sport. Competition by its very nature, these critics would maintain, cannot satisfy ethical requirements. Let us consider this view in some depth.

### Competition and Selfishness

Perhaps the most important criticism of the moral worth of competition is that competition is selfish and egoistic. Since competitive activities are zero-sum games, one person's victory is another's defeat. As we have seen, the internal goal of competition is to ensure victory for oneself and defeat for one's opponent.

According to some critics, such as political theorist John Schaar, the competitive society is not a very attractive place. It reduces human interaction to "a context in which each man competes with his fellows for scarce goods, a contest in which there is never enough for everybody, and where one man's gain is usually another's loss."[15] This position is forcefully defended by Michael Fielding, a thoughtful writer on educational philosophy, who maintains that

> I reject the use of competition in schools. . . . part of one's characterization contains some reference to working against others in a spirit of selfishness; for that reason I would also deplore any fostering of a competitive motive; the act of competing is thus irremediably objectionable as is the social ideal which forms a substantial part of the political backcloth against which such practices are set.[16]

The argument of the critics, then, is roughly this. The goal of competition is enhancement of the position of one competitor at the expense of others. Thus, by its very nature, the goal of competition is selfish. But since selfish concern for oneself at the expense of others is immoral, it follows that competition is immoral as well.

This argument surely is not without intuitive force since in athletic competition, if X wins then Y loses and X tries to attain victory over Y. Nevertheless, even if the assertion that competition is essentially selfish turns out to be justifiable when applied to society at large, which is open to doubt, it faces special difficulties when applied to sports and athletics.

For one thing, the idea of competition in sports as a virtually unrestricted war of all against all seems vastly overdrawn. If team sports involve competition between opponents, they also involve cooperation among members of the same team. Moreover, in many sports, including some forms of professional athletics, it is not uncommon for opponents to give each other help in the form of instruction before contests. Thus, one widely cited explanation for the slump of professional golfer Ben Crenshaw during the early 1980s was the oversolicitiousness of his fellow golf professionals, who bombarded him with remedies (which many feel only confused him even further). This kind of help which opponents sometimes provide to one another, although unintelligible if we regard athletic competition as a kind of war, makes perfect sense if its value lies in facing the challenge good competition provides.

In addition, as we have noted, competition in sport takes place within a framework of constitutive rules binding on all participants. The ideal of good competition requires competitors to forego momentary advantages which might be obtained by violation of the rules. Commitment to this ideal is illustrated by weekend tennis players and top tournament golfers who call penalties on themselves, sometimes at great financial cost. In other sports, officials are charged with enforcing rules. But while it is considered legitimate to question the judgment of such officials, no one can legitimately protest that the officials ought not to apply the rules in the first place.

At this point, critics might concede that there are some restraints on selfishness in athletic competition. But, they might retort that just as limited war is still war, so too is constrained selfishness a form of selfishness.

However, this rejoinder may be questionable if we apply the distinction made earlier between the internal goals of an activity and the primary motive of the participants for engaging in it. Competitors need not have as their primary motive the desire to beat opponents. Although as good competitors they try their best to win, they may value the competition not primarily for its outcome but for the process of testing oneself against other athletes.

Consider the following description of a Yale-Princeton football game played in 1895. Princeton was winning 16-10 but Yale was right on the Princeton goal line with a chance to turn the tide on the very last play of the game.

> The clamor ceased once absolutely, and the silence was even more impressive than the tumult that had preceded it. . . . While they (Yale) were lining up for that last effort the cheering died away, yells both measured and inarticulate stopped and the place was so still . . . you could hear the telegraph instruments chirping like crickets from the side.[17]

Yale scores to win the game on a brilliant run.

> It is not possible to describe that run. It would be as easy to explain how a snake disappears through the grass, or an eel slips from your fingers, or to say how a flash of linked lightning wriggles across the sky.[18]

Is the important point here simply that Yale won and Princeton lost? Edwin Delattre, one of our wisest educators, draws a different lesson from this episode and the many like it that take place during all seasons and at different levels of athletic competition.

> Such moments are what makes the game worth the candle. Whether amidst the soft lights and sparkling balls against the baize of a billiard table, or the rolling terrain of a lush fairway or in the violent and crashing pits where linemen struggle, it is the moments when no let up is possible, when there is virtually no tolerance for error, which make up the game. The best and most satisfying contests maximize these moments and minimize respite from pressure.[19]

According to Delattre, it is these moments of test rather than victory or defeat that are the source of the value of competition in sport.

> The testing of one's mettle in competitive athletics is a form of self discovery. . . . The claim of competitive athletics to importance rests squarely on their providing us opportunities for self discovery which might otherwise have been missed. . . . They provide opportunities for self-discovery, for concentration and intensity of involvement, for being carried away by the demands of the contest . . . with a frequency seldom matched elsewhere. . . . This is why it is a far greater success in competitive athletics to have played well under pressure of a truly worthwhile opponent and lost than to have defeated a less worthy or unworthy one where no demands were made.[20]

Delattre would argue, then, that although it is essential to good competition that the competitors try as hard as they can to achieve victory, the principal value of athletic competition lies not in the attainment of victory itself but in the process of trying to overcome a worthy opponent. This position suggests that we can view competition as significantly *cooperative* rather than as a purely selfish zero-sum game. Opponents are engaging in the *cooperative* enterprise of generating challenges against which they can test themselves. Each has the obligation to the other to try his or her best. Although one wins and the other loses, each gains by facing a test that each voluntarily chooses to undertake.

At this point, opponents of competition in sport may become impatient. "Delattre has shown that competition is not selfish," they might retort, "only by the verbal trick of redefining it so that it is no longer genuine competition at all." What such critics may have in mind is this: If what is important about competition is what individuals learn about themselves through response to challenge, athletic contests can be viewed as means to self-knowledge and self-improvement. Individuals need not try to win but only to do the best they can under pressure. The aim is no longer to defeat an opponent but to achieve personal growth. At most, what we have is "competition with oneself," not competition with others. Thus, according to the criticism we are considering, Delattre has not succeeded in defending competition in sport. Rather, he has replaced it with the goal of self-development.

### Competition with Self

The expression "competition with self" calls up the image of athletes playing against ghostly images of their earlier selves. Since there are no ghostly images and no presently existing earlier self to compete against, the expression "competition with self," if not downright incoherent, is seriously misleading. It will be clearer and less paradoxical to speak of individuals striving for self-improvement rather than speaking loosely of competing against oneself.

Should participants in sport strive only for self-improvement? Is sport, viewed as a means for self-improvement, of greater value or more ethically defensible than competitive athletics?

Before turning directly to these questions, we should first consider if Delattre's defense of competition in sport is really a disguised shift away from a competitive ideal towards one of self-improvement. While each approach repudiates the view that winning is everything in sports, Delattre's position emphasizes not just improvement but improvement in meeting *challenges set by an opponent.* As many have found out to their sorrow, there is a major difference between showing improvement in a sport under relaxed practice conditions and rising to the challenge once a competitive contest has begun. Indeed, if we are relatively inexperienced or inexpert, we may pass the test of competition even if our performance is below our best level but is reasonably good, given the pressure of the situation.

This suggests that competition in sport, understood as the mutual quest for excellence in the face of challenge, differs significantly from the effort to improve. One can strive to improve without striving to demonstrate improvement under competitive fire, and care about meeting competitive challenges consistently without trying to improve overall performance. Moreover, *one approach does not rule out the other.* Individuals can participate in sports and athletics with the desire to improve *and* the desire to meet the challenges set by an opponent. Indeed, one might aim to improve precisely at performing well under competitive pressure.

Competition as the mutual quest for excellence in meeting challenge (henceforth referred to simply as the mutual quest for excellence) is not equivalent to the quest for self-improvement. However, the two may share a number of related features.

For one thing, an especially significant criterion of improvement is change in one's competitive standing when measured against the performance of others. A major—perhaps the best—way to tell if one is improving is to see if one does better against opponents than one has done in the past.

But doing better against others is not merely a contingent sign of improvement. In many contexts in sports, what counts as playing well will be logically determined by what counts as an appropriate response to the moves of opponents. For example, it would be incorrect to say that Jones played well in a tennis match if what Jones did was hit crisp ground strokes in a situation where intelligent play called for charging the net.

Indeed, even in sports that need not be played against a human opponent, such as running or golf, improvement cannot easily be divorced from comparison with the achievements of others. Robert Nozick provides a pertinent illustration.

> A man living in an isolated mountain village can sink 15 jump shots with a basketball out of 150 tries. Everyone else in the village can sink only one jump shot out of 150 tries. He thinks (as do the others) that he's very good at it. One day along comes Jerry West.[21]

The example illustrates that what counts as a significant achievement requires reference to the performance of others. What may not be so obvious is that *improvement* depends in a similar way upon comparative judgments about ability. Before the arrival of a great professional basketball player such as Jerry West, the villager may have thought that improving his average to 17 out of 150 shots would constitute improvement of a significant order. After the visit, even if it is acknowledged that no one in the village can ever equal West's skills, the very criterion of significant improvement will have changed. At the very least, the more expert villagers should expect that after practice they should make 20 or 30 shots out of 150 tries. Before the visit, the 20-shot barrier must have seemed as impossible to reach as breaking the 4-minute mile seemed to runners of an earlier era.

Does it follow, then, that if an athlete is concerned with self-improvement, he or she is implicitly competing with others? Such an athlete is striving to reach standards set by an appropriate reference group of other athletes. Thus, success or failure is at least partially determined by the performances of others. Accordingly, those who value "competition with self" because it seems not to involve (possibly negative) comparisons with the performance of others may need to rethink their position.

On the other hand, there is a difference between competition and self-improvement as ideals of good sport. The attainment of high standards of improvement by one participant does not preclude attainment by others. In competition, however, only one player or team can win in any contest. Moreover, competition emphasizes the challenge constituted by an opponent, while improvement emphasizes the development of skills rather than response to another's play. There are important differences, then, between the ideal of self-improvement and the ideal of competition as the mutual quest for excellence. But we have seen that there are important resemblances between the two as well.

Even if there is a sharper conceptual distinction between the two ideals than suggested above, it is far from clear that they should be kept distinct in practice. Suppose for example that airline pilots were given the following advice.

> Don't worry about whether you are good or bad pilots. Just try to get better and better every day.

Surely both passengers and pilots have a right to know not just whether individual pilots are improving but also what level of achievement each individual actually has attained. Similarly, if athletic achievement is regarded as significant, and surely the athlete who strives to improve does regard it as significant, participants may have a claim to know how good they are at their sport.[22] That evaluation, in turn, is not easily separable from a comparison with the achievements of others.

To summarize, there are good reasons for accepting each of the following propositions.

> Competition with self, in the sense of the quest for self-improvement, is distinguishable from competition in sport. In particular, while not all participants can win, all can reach their highest potential.

> Neither competition nor the quest for improvement rules out the need for comparison with the performances of others.

> Competing with oneself does not preclude competing against others. Competition with self, in the sense of the quest for self-improvement, is compatible with the goal of meeting competitive challenges. Athletes, therefore, can seek to attain both goals and need not choose between them.

Why shouldn't we pursue *both* improvement and competitive excellence? Once we see that "competition with oneself," properly understood, involves comparison with the performance of others, there seems to be little reason to commit ourselves totally to one goal at the expense of the other.

### Selfishness Revisited

So far, it has been suggested that athletic competition, conceived of as a mutual quest for excellence in the face of an opponent's challenge, contains significant cooperative elements. Each opponent, on this conception, has an obligation to do his or her best so as to provide the best possible challenge for the other opponent. Keeping this conception in mind, let us consider once again the charge that the desire to achieve victory—which can only be achieved by defeating an opponent—is essentially selfish.

It is true that winning normally will be in a competitor's self-interest. However, it need not always be so. Winning may generate excessive self-confidence, and may lead to the manifestation of egotistical behavior which ultimately loses friends and wins enemies. Whether or not winning is in one's self-interest in particular cases is an empirical question, depending upon the particular circumstances at hand.

However, even if victory is in one's *self-interest*, it does not follow that the pursuit of victory is *selfish*. A great deal will depend on what we mean by "selfish." Of course, if we define selfish behavior as self-interested behavior, then the pursuit of victory will be selfish whenever it is in the competitor's self-interest. But is such a characterization of selfishness acceptable?

Consider the following examples.

Jones is playing in a touch football game with friends. Jones says, "I'll be the quarterback." The others declare that they too want to be quarterbacks and suggest the position be shared. Jones replies, "Its my football! If you don't let me be quarterback, I'll take my ball and go home."

Jones is in a spelling contest between two teams in his fifth grade class. He correctly spells a difficult word. As a result, his team wins and the other team loses.

Surely the concept of selfishness is stretched too far if it is used to apply to both kinds of cases. Isn't there a significant difference between the first case, in which Jones *disregards* the interests of others in favor of his own, and the second case, in which each student is given a fair chance to succeed? If there is an important difference between trying to defeat an opponent within a mutually acceptable framework of rules and simply disregarding the interests of others, then there is an important difference between athletic competition and selfish behavior. At the very least, the charge that trying to win is inherently selfish presupposes a questionable account of selfishness; one which may not stand up to the critical scrutiny of further discussion and inquiry.

To summarize, the charge that competition in sports and athletics is essentially selfish faces several objections. It does not assign adequate weight to cooperative elements in competition, particularly the extent to which competition may be a *mutual* quest for excellence. Finally, it rests on a questionable account of selfishness itself. Accordingly, while the ultimate force of these points needs to be determined by further discussion, perhaps enough has been said to warrant some scepticism toward the charge that competition in sports is just another example of selfish acquisitiveness in action.

### Competition and Inequality

While some opponents of competition in sports emphasize its alleged selfishness, others are concerned about the kind of inequality they find essential to competition. On their view, competition, by its very nature, is inequitable. It divides us into winners and losers, successes and failures, stars and scrubs. Many of us are all too familiar with the slogans, popular with some coaches, which equate losing with total failure and assign "losers" to an inferior branch of the human race.

In fact, competition is too often used as the basis for invidious distinctions. Making an error in a ball game is equated with lack of drive or cowardice. In the earlier stages of his career, golfer Tom Watson was referred to as a "choker" because he couldn't seem to hold leads in tournaments. He later buried this label by winning many major championships. One of the sadder features of organized sports for children is the emphasis sometimes placed on winning by the adults involved. As a result, young players often become more concerned with avoiding errors than with enjoying competition or developing fundamental skills.

It is arguable, however, that such attitudes reflect *excessive* emphasis on winning and are not essential to competition itself. The winners of an athletic contest need not be viewed as "winners" in any larger sense and losers need not be bad or inferior persons.

Nevertheless, to the extent that winning is regarded as an achievement, distinctions will be made. In the higher levels of amateur competition, as well as among the professionals, winning will lead to an unequal distribution of fame and fortune. What *principles* can be applied here to determine whether or not such distinctions are unfair?

It will be useful to employ a distinction made by the legal scholar, Ronald Dworkin. Dworkin suggests that we distinguish between the right to *equal treatment*, "which is the right to an equal distribution of some opportunity or resource or burden" and the right to *treatment as an equal,* which is the right "to be treated with the same respect or concern as anyone else."[23] Equal respect and concern do not necessarily involve equal outcomes, in the sense of identical distribution of some good. Thus, if one of my children is sick and the other is well, equal treatment, in the sense of dividing the available medicine strictly in half, is not required by the right to treatment as an equal. Rather, provision of all the medicine to the sick child is compatible with and may be required by equal respect and concern for both children.[24]

This suggests, as Dworkin himself maintains, that treatment as an equal is a more fundamental right than equal treatment. Unequal outcomes are not unjust or inequitable if they reflect or are compatible with equal respect and concern for persons. Unequal result, in the sense of different result, is not necessarily unjust.

Accordingly, while competition does lead to unequal treatment in the sense of unequal result, this is not sufficient to show that competition is unfair or unjust. The critic must show not just that there is a distinction between winners and losers but that this distinction somehow is unfair, perhaps because it violates the right to treatment *as* an equal.

Contrary to the critic, it is arguable that if people are treated as equals, with equal respect and concern, justified inequalities of result naturally will emerge. This is because part of treating persons with respect surely is treating them as beings "who are capable of forming and acting on intelligent conceptions of how their lives should be lived."[25] But different people will have different conceptions of how their lives should be led and make different choices accordingly. For example, if more critics respond favorably to one novel than to another, the author of the first may become more famous and more wealthy than the author of the second. But how can such an inequality be avoided without prohibiting persons from making and acting upon their critical judgments; by failing to respect and treat them as persons?[26]

A similar case can be made for the view that the kinds of inequality of outcome which result from competition in sport also can be justified by appeal to the right to treatment as an equal and the value of respecting persons as such. For one thing, most participants in athletic competition are there because they want to be competing. They themselves find the challenge posed by competitors worth meeting and the activity of competition worth their commitment. If respect for persons requires that we respect their conception of how their life should be led—as long as it involves no violation of the rights of others—the inequalities of outcome generated by competition in sport seem no less justified than other inequalities which arise from the uncoerced autonomous choices of those involved.

Critics might object that treating people as equals involves more than simply respecting their choices. Suppose Jones chooses to continually humiliate himself in an attempt to gain Smith's affections. Surely Smith does not treat Jones with respect if she continually heaps humiliation upon him, even though he himself chooses to leave himself open to such treatment. Rather, Jones is degrading himself, and Smith is contributing to his degradation. Similarly, just because competitors agree to compete, it doesn't follow that they are being treated as equals through competition. In addition, it must be shown that the competitive relationship itself is not inherently degrading or incompatible in some other way with respect for persons as equals.

Indeed, the competitive relationship often is characterized in derogatory terms. Competitors are seen as mere obstacles to be overcome, rather than as fellow participants and persons. They are to be "destroyed," "humiliated," "trampled over," or "run off the court." Persons are reduced to mere things; barriers which stand in the way of personal success.

For example, in a major college football game, a star running back, playing again for the first time after a serious knee injury, reported that during a pile up, he felt one of the opponents twisting his knee. Thinking quickly, he yelled out, "You've got the wrong knee! You've got the wrong knee!"[27]

If the competitive attitude required that we attempt to injure our opponents, it would be ethically indefensible. It should be clear from our earlier discussion, however, that the ethics of good competition prohibits the intentional infliction of injury. If competition is most defensibly understood as the mutual quest for excellence, one should want opponents to be at their peak so as to present the best challenge possible. Victory, if it is to be significant, requires *outplaying* worthy opponents, not eliminating them.

Accordingly, in evaluating competition in sport, it is crucial that features that are essential or central to competition be distinguished from those that are not. Proponents of the value of competition in sport can use this distinction to argue that many objectionable features of actual competitive practice are inessential to competition as such. In particular, the reduction of opposing players to mere things, while unfortunately too often a part of high pressure athletics, is not a necessary element of competitive sport and can consistently be condemned by proponents of a defensible competitive ethic.

Participants in competitive sport, as we have seen, presumably prefer a life which includes competition, with the possibility of winning or losing, to a life that does not. Moreover, within athletics, participants exercise choice about what skills are to be developed, what strategies are to be employed, and what commitments to training and practice are to be made and honored. If treating individuals as equals requires us to react appropriately to their choices, to treat them as agents "capable of forming and acting on an intelligent conception of how their lives should be lived,"[28] inequalities that arise from their decisions in athletics are presumptively fair and equitable.

An even stronger conclusion is supported by our discussion. Since within athletic competition each competitor must respond and react to the *actions* of other persons—actions which manifest the skills the participants have chosen to develop and the decisions they have made during play—competition in sport is a paradigm case of an activity in which the participants treat each other as equals. Each player respects and responds to the choices of others. The good competitor, then, does not see an opponent as a thing to be overcome but as a person whose activity calls for appropriate response. Thus, rather than being incompatible with equal respect for persons, competition in athletics, at its best, may presuppose it.

### Conclusions

Competition in the context of sports has been defended as a mutually acceptable quest for excellence. Excellence is to be attained through the response to challenges created by an opponent. Since the quest is for challenge in the realm of sports and athletics, it is a quest for excellence in the intelligent, directed use of physical talents. Our discussion suggests that since competition is a *mutual* quest which respects our moral status as persons, the charges of selfishness and inequity sometimes directed against it are unfounded.

This has implications for evaluation of the utilitarian arguments discussed earlier. In assessing the effects of competitive sports, we would do well to distinguish the effects of those practices which deviate from the ethic of the mutual quest for excellence from those that conform to it. Perhaps critics of competitive sports concentrate on the former while adherents concentrate on the latter. If so, neither side is wholly right or wrong. Rather, the moral of the story will be that we can obtain more beneficial results by reforming actual practice so that it conforms more closely to our ideal principles.

This does not imply, however, that all sports should involve intense competition. Not everyone wants a challenge, at least not all the time. Individuals who find enough challenge in other areas, such as their work, may prefer to play noncompetitively or not play at all. However, in so far as an activity is a sport, it is parasitic on the mutual quest for excellence, even if the players avoid any high degree of competitive intensity. This is because their goal *qua* players is still to make correct moves or plays, even if they do not attach great significance to success or failure. If standards of good and bad performance did not apply, they would be engaging in mere exercise and not sport.

This suggests that some critics of overemphasis on competition may ignore perhaps equally deleterious effects of underemphasis. Thus, if participants normally are told, "It doesn't matter how you do, just go out and have fun," the subtle message being conveyed may be that doing well is unimportant. If participation in competitive sport can be a form of human excellence and if it can contribute to self-development and reinforce desirable character traits, one may not want to convey the impression that performance doesn't matter.

Of course, we should sometimes play just for fun. But perhaps the proper attitude toward competition is captured neither by "Winning is everything" or "Just have fun; how you do doesn't matter," but rather by "Try your best; the fun is in the trying." The trick for coaches and educators is to strike the right balance between emphasis on achievement and emphasis on participation for the age group and stage of athletic development of the individuals involved. (See Chapter Five for a fuller discussion of these points.)

So far, we have been concerned with the ethics of good competition. However, we still need to consider the importance of winning. In particular, what are the implications of the model of competitive sport as the mutual quest for excellence on the importance of securing victory and avoiding defeat in competitive athletics?

## IS WINNING IMPORTANT?

If we view competitive sports and athletics as a mutual quest for excellence in the face of challenge, one might argue that success in meeting the challenges posed by opponents is important. Winning is significant, on this view, because winning is the criterion of success. To lose is to fail to meet the challenge, while to win is to succeed. Accordingly, while winning may not be everything, it surely is something. If competition is viewed as a quest for challenge, importance surely should be assigned to whether or not the challenge is met. After all, the principal point of deliberately creating a difficult task for oneself is to see if one can accomplish it.

It doesn't follow, however, that winning is invariably a sign of success or losing invariably a sign of failure. If winning were the only criterion of success, it would be sensible to take pride in consistently defeating weaker opponents by lopsided margins. One could achieve success all the time simply by scheduling competitive inferiors. Conversely, if losing were an invariable criterion of failure, a weaker opponent would have no cause for pride after having extended a far superior competitor to the limit before going down to ultimate defeat.

This suggests that winning is not everything. Through trying to win, each competitor generates a challenge to the other, but it is possible that *each* competitor meets the challenge although one wins and one loses.

However, this does not imply that who wins or who loses is unimportant. For one thing, while it is easy enough to make excuses, such as "We played very well but lost to a clearly better team," one may secretly suspect that the truth is, "If we had played to our real potential, we would have won." What looks like meeting the challenge may be a surface appearance only. More important, playing well in some aesthetic sense may not entail playing well competitively. Recall our earlier example of the tennis player who hits beautiful ground strokes when a more aggressive game at the net is called for by the strategic situation. It may be the competitive situation that dictates what counts as a good play. A beautifully swished 25-foot jump shot may make no competitive sense if the shooter's team is tied for the lead with 15 seconds left on the clock. What might look from an aesthetic standpoint like superb performance might simply count as unintelligent play from the competitive point of view. Thus, while winning is not an invariable criterion of competitive success, it often will be a reliable sign of it.

Moreover, when opponents are evenly matched, victory may be virtually indistinguishable from competitive success. Since one is trying to meet the challenge set by the opponent, why shouldn't one feel disappointed by losing or elated by winning? Even when opponents are mismatched, pride in victory may be called for. The victors may be pleased that they managed to perform well even without the incentive of facing a strong opponent.

Accordingly, while success and failure in competitive sport cannot be identified with winning and losing, winning and losing often will be principal indicators of success and failure. In many competitive contexts, it won't do to separate winning and losing from how well one played the game, because the outcome of the game is one important measure of how well one actually played.

But why should success and failure matter at all? After all, "it's only a game."

If the slogan "It's only a game" means that extreme depression, abusiveness to friends, spouse beating, sullen withdrawal, and existential anxiety are inappropriate responses to defeat in athletics, it surely is correct. Sports are activities through which we have fun, develop our potentialities, and learn to enjoy meeting challenges; they are not matters of life and death.

On the other hand, if "It's only a game" means that success and failure in competitive sport doesn't matter at all, it is far more dubious. While sports surely lack the cosmic significance of fine art, drama, science, or philosophy, they are not insignificant. On the contrary, they provide a context in which we can stretch our bodily skills and capacities as agents to their limits in the pursuit of excellence. If a critic responds, "Why should anyone even care about excellence in sports?" the beginnings of a proper response would be that the pursuit of excellence in the use of the body hardly is trivial. To the contrary, the meeting of the demands athletes place upon their talents often involves beauty, courage, dedication, and excitement. If those things don't matter, what should? Finally, at the professional level, concern for professional success, which may involve winning, is no less appropriate than similar concern in other professions.

Accordingly, if one defends competition in sport as the mutual quest for excellence in the face of challenge, one is committed to the view that outcomes do matter. While winning and losing are at best imperfect indicators of competitive success or failure, the whole point of developing and testing skills is to try to meet the test set by an opponent's play. The pursuit of excellence in sport matters, on this view, not only because of alleged good consequences, such as character development, which it might promote. Rather, it also is of *intrinsic worth* since the pursuit of excellence in sport is a paradigm activity in which we function as responsible, autonomous agents, as persons who are to be respected as equals.

It is worth considering, here, William Bennett's description of a rigidly noncompetitive softball team he refers to as the Persons.

> The team is co-ed, they have no "discrimination" and no "rules".
> . . . Occasionally, they let one of their dogs . . . "play a position" . . .
> and the Persons laugh and try to look loose and non-competitive. . . .
> In the end, the Persons must be judged in their own terms to be insensitive,
> both to the game and to one another as "players"—the cost no doubt of each
> one's being sensitive to himself exclusively as a Person.[29]

Bennett concludes that

> Charles Reich's ideal in *The Greening of America*—a laughing generation
> playing football in bell bottom trousers—is one of sheer aimlessness, of
> distraction pure and simple, doing nothing. Serious playing and watching,

on the other hand, . . . are rarely if ever doing nothing, for sports is a way to scorn indifference, and occasionally, indeed, one can even discern in competition those elements of grace, skill, beauty and courage that mirror the greatest affirmations of human spirit and passion.[30]

## SUMMARY

This chapter suggests that competition in the context of sports is most defensible ethically when understood as a mutual quest for excellence in the face of challenge in the intelligent and directed use of athletic skills. Competition in sports, under appropriate conditions, may have such beneficial consequences as manifesting and reinforcing our commitment to certain values and personal virtues. Most important, it may be of *intrinsic* worth as a framework within which we express ourselves as persons and respond to others as such in the pursuit of excellence. While other such frameworks exist, few are as universally accessible and involve us so fully as agents who must use their bodies to meet challenges we have chosen for ourselves.

Competition as the mutual quest for excellence, it must be emphasized, is an *ideal*. Actual practices may not conform to such an ideal. In the real world, winning may be overemphasized, the wrong values may be manifested, and the spirit of selfishness may reign supreme. If so, the ideal provides grounds for criticizing actual behavior which deviates substantially from it. In the remainder of this book, the ideal will be applied to the moral evaluation of actual practices in sport.

The ideal presented here needs itself to be examined, refined, criticized, or even replaced if substantial enough objections are raised against it. However, without some defensible standards against which current practices can be measured, the valuable aspects of such activities cannot be distinguished from the harmful or unfair aspects. Without standards of evaluation, criticism and acclaim alike would rest on purely emotive reactions rather than upon the results of perhaps the most important quest; the quest for justification through meeting the challenges of open discussion and critical inquiry.

## NOTES

[1]What Lombardi is claimed to have actually said is "winning isn't everything, but wanting to win is." Scott Morris, ed., *The Book of Strange Facts and Useless Information* (New York: Dolphin, 1979).

[2]The statement by Rice is from *John Bartlett's Familiar Quotations* (Boston: Little, Brown and Co., 1951), p. 901, while the remark by Evashevski is from *Sports Illustrated*, Sept. 23, 1957, p. 119. For discussion, see James W. Keating, "Winning in Sports and Athletics," *Thought*, Vol. 38, No. 149, 1963, pp. 201-210.

[3]Gerald Eskanazi, "Judy Cooperstein Still Has the Tempo." *The New York Times*, July 2, 1981, p. B12. © 1981 by The New York Times Company. Reprinted by permission.

[4]For discussion of an alleged distinction between sports and athletics, see Keating, "Winning in Sports and Athletics." In that essay, Keating argues that

> Sport is a kind of diversion which has for its direct and immediate end, fun, pleasure and delight. . . . Athletics, on the other hand, is essentially a competitive activity, which has for its end, victory . . . and which is characterized by a spirit of dedication, sacrifice and intensity. (pp. 204–205)

Keating can best be understood here as distinguishing two attitudes towards participation in sport and not two kinds of activities. Thus, fishing is a sport which can be engaged in competitively, as in contests. In such contests, anglers are not suddenly transformed into athletes, a status which they failed to attain until they fished competitively. I use "sports" and "athletics" interchangeably unless some difference is made explicit in the surrounding text.

[5]Ludwig Wittgenstein has suggested there are *no* elements common to all games in his *Philosophical Investigations* (New York: Macmillan, 1953). For a particularly delightful and extended defense of a formal definition of "game," see Bernard Suits, *The Grasshopper: Games, Life and Utopia* (Toronto: The University of Toronto Press, 1978).

[6]For an argument that any attempt to define "competition" will be ideologically loaded see Michael Fielding, "Against Competition," *Proceedings of the Philosophy of Education Society of Great Britain*, Vol. X, July, 1976, pp. 124–146.

[7]See Suits, *The Grasshopper: Games, Life and Utopia*. While games won by illegal but unintentional and unnoticed moves, such as the kicking of a field goal with an extra player on the football field, may present a problem for this analysis, arguably those who knowingly and intentionally depart from the rules do not really win, since they do not truly play the game at all.

[8]John Loy and Gerald S. Kenyon, *Sport, Culture and Society* (New York: Macmillan, 1969), pp. 9–10, quoted by Harry Edwards in his *Sociology of Sport* (Homewood, Ill.: The Dorsey Press, 1973), p. 88.

[9]M. M. Hussey, "Character Education in Athletics," *The American Educational Review*, Vol. 33, 1938, p. 578, quoted by Edwards, *Sociology of Sport*, p. 94.

[10]Bruce C. Ogilvie and Thomas Tutko, "Sports: If You Want to Build Character, Try Something Else," *Psychology Today*, Oct. 1971, pp. 61–62. Reprinted from *Psychology Today* Magazine copyright 1971.

[11]Ibid., p. 61.

[12]Walter E. Schafer, "Some Social Sources and Consequences of Interscholastic Athletics," in Gerald Kenyon, ed., *The Sociology of Sport* (Chicago: The Athletic Institute, 1969), p. 35, quoted by Edwards, *Sociology of Sport*, p. 324.

[13]This is suggested by Edwards, *Sociology of Sport*, p. 323.

[14]The idea of an "expressive" theory is suggested by Joel Feinberg's "The Expressive Function of Punishment" in his *Doing and Deserving* (Princeton, N.J.: Princeton University Press, 1970), pp. 95–118. Feinberg himself does not discuss the expressive function of sports.

[15]John Schaar, "Equality of Opportunity and Beyond," in J. Roland Pennock and John W. Chapman, eds., *Equality*, Nomos IX (New York: Atherton Press, 1967), p. 237.

[16]Fielding, "Against Competition," pp. 140–141.

[17]Richard Harding Davis, "Thorne's Famous Run," in Grantland Rice and Harford Powel, eds., *The Omnibus of Sport* (New York: Harper and Brothers, 1932), reprinted from "How the Great Game was Played," *The Journal*, Nov. 24, 1895, quoted by Edwin J. Delattre, "Some Reflections on Success and Failure in Competitive Athletics," *Journal of the Philosophy of Sport*, Vol. II, 1975, pp. 134–135.

[18]Delattre, Ibid., pp. 134–135.

[19]Delattre, Ibid., p. 134.

[20]Delattre, Ibid., p. 135.

[21]Robert Nozick, *Anarchy, State and Utopia* (New York: Basic Books, 1974), p. 240.

[22]For discussion of a similar point regarding assignments of grades to students, see Steven M. Cahn, *Education and the Democratic Ideal* (Chicago: Nelson-Hall, 1979), Chapters 7-10.

[23]Ronald Dworkin, *Taking Rights Seriously* (Cambridge: Harvard University Press, 1977), p. 227.

[24]Dworkin uses this kind of example to illustrate the same point in *Taking Rights Seriously*, p. 227.

[25]Ibid., p. 272.

[26]For a fuller defense of the view that meritocratic practices can be defended by appeal to the requirement of respect for persons, see Robert L. Simon, "Equality, Merit and the Determination of Our Gifts," *Social Research*, Autumn, 1974, pp. 492–514 and "An Indirect Defense of the Merit Principle," *The Philosophical Forum*, Vol. X, No. 2-4, 1978–1979, pp. 224–241.

[27]Quoted from memory of a postgame interview.

[28]Dworkin, *Taking Rights Seriously*, p. 272.

[29]William J. Bennett, "In Defense of Sports," *Commentary*, Vol. 61, No. 2, 1976, p. 70. Reprinted from *Commentary*, February 1976, by permission; all rights reserved.

[30] Ibid.

# CHAPTER THREE
# ETHICS IN COMPETITION
## Violence in sports

On Lincoln's Birthday 1982, under the photograph of Vito Romero, Benjamin Davis and Louis Wade walked into the Civic Auditorium in Albuquerque to fight each other in the semi-finals of the New Mexico Golden Gloves, a 132 pound novice class. You could not hope to meet two nicer boys. One would help kill the other in the ring that night.[1]

Benjamin Davis, known as Benjii, and Louis Wade had never met before that tragic night in 1982. Although Benjii was 22 and Louis only 16, they had much in common. They were regarded as fine young men by those who knew them. They were loved by their families. They participated in boxing, not because they wanted to become professionals or because they wanted to hurt anyone, but because they wanted to work out and because they enjoyed the competition.

Although the boys came from different ethnic backgrounds—Benjii was a Navajo while Louis was Anglo—they had much in common. They loved sports and were hard-working students. "But here they were, alone, prepared only to hit each other, to entertain a few thousand people who had come to pass the time on a Friday evening on Lincoln's birthday watching brave boys rattle each other's young brains."[2]

The tragedy happened in the second round. Benjii received a number of hard blows and seemed dazed, but the referee did not stop the fight. More blows followed and Benjii appeared even more dazed.

Again Louis held back. There was no sign from the referee even though when Benjii righted himself, Louis could see that his eyes were glassy. But Benjii was back on his two feet now, and the crowd was cheering and Louis fired one more time, another left. This time Benjii crumpled and fell in a heap on the canvas, his brain now swimming in blood, bruised and purple and of no more use to him.[3]

Benjii never recovered. Apparently no one in his family blames Louis for what happened. "To this day they only have compassion for him, and everybody keeps assuring Louis that it was not his fault. Sometimes he believes that."[4]

Surely Louis is not to blame for Benjii's tragic death. He played by the rules in a sport which involved an element of risk to both participants. But is the sport itself morally acceptable? Should our society permit young men to participate in such a violent activity, let alone make heroes out of the most successful of the competitors?

More than 350 boxers have been killed in the ring since 1945. The risks are borne not only by professional boxers, who sometimes fight for huge rewards, but by boys and young men such as Louis and Benjii. Even boxers who live to a ripe old age often suffer such effects of cumulative brain damage as the stumbling walk and memory lapses of the "punch-drunk" fighter.

The problems raised by the apparent use of violence in sport are not restricted to boxing. Serious injuries and death occur in other contact sports, as a direct result of the roughness which is a necessary element of the games being played. Death or paralysis is not infrequently the result of neck injuries suffered in football. Attempts at physical intimidation of opposing players by "enforcers" may sometimes lead to crippling injuries on the gridiron. The now familiar joke to the effect that "I went to a fight the other night and a hockey game broke out" says something significant about the level of violence in professional hockey.

Violence in sport is an increasing problem. According to many observers of American sport, it is on the rise not only on the field but among spectators as well.[5] Does violence on the field or in the ring contribute to violence in the stands? What is the place of violence in sports? Is boxing immoral? Should hockey be reformed? Is football intrinsically violent and therefore morally objectionable?

In Chapter Two, we considered the moral status of competition in sports and athletics. The conclusion that emerged from the discussion was that athletic competition, conceived of as a mutually acceptable quest for excellence among opponents, is not only permissible but may also have special value as an expression of our status as persons.

However, we did not investigate the ethics that should apply *within* competition. That is, we considered whether athletic competition could be defended against external attack, not how ethical problems internal to competition might be resolved.

In this chapter, we will examine certain ethical questions about the role of violence in sport. These questions explore the scope and limits of the competitive ethic developed earlier. As we will see, the issues raised are not only about sport but also are about the meaning of liberty, the relationship between society and the individual, and the significance of respect for persons.

## THE ROLE OF VIOLENCE IN SPORTS

Many questions can be asked about the role of violence in sports. For example, one can ask the empirical question about how much violence there is in sport and what factors contribute to it. One can also ask the moral question about when, if ever, violence in sports in permissible. Such questions presuppose that the concept of violence is a clear one. If, on the contrary, there are different conceptions of violence, the questions themselves will be ambiguous. Since not all those asking the questions will mean the same thing by "violence," their questions, while apparently similar at a superficial level, will really be different. Although all the questioners will be using the word "violence," they will not mean the same thing by it. It is important, then, that we be clear when assessing any claims about violence just which conception of violence is being employed.

### Conceptions of Violence

Examples of violence unfortunately are everywhere about us. Clearly, if one person assaults another, a violent act has taken place. But how is "violence" itself to be characterized. Are brushback pitches or hard tackles just as much instances of violence as an assault?

Violence generally involves the use of force, but not every use of force is violent. For example, a tennis player uses force in serving but few of us would characterize a serve in tennis as an act of violence. Indeed, it is possible that some acts—such as intense verbal abuse—might be characterized as instances of (psychological) violence without involving the use of force at all. So violence and the use of force cannot be equated.

Can violence be characterized as the *wrongful* use of force? Leaving aside possible cases of psychological violence, which might not involve force, other difficulties arise. The proposed account of violence is morally loaded. That is, before we can determine whether any particular act is a violent one, we must first determine whether the act is morally wrong. What we characterize as violence depends on our moral views. Thus, if we believe that the use of force by the Allies in World War II was justified, we would not be able to call the Allied war effort violent. Surely, that is absurd. Indeed, if violence is by definition wrong, we would first have to agree on which conduct is wrong before we could decide whether or not it is violent. But surely that is putting the cart before the horse. Often, we are certain that some particular act is violent even if we are unsure whether it is right or wrong. Indeed, we may regard it as wrong precisely *because* it is violent, which would be impossible if we first had to decide an act was wrong before we could describe it as violent. For example, we may think that an assault is wrong precisely because of the injury done to the victim, rather than decide the assault was violent because it was wrong on independent grounds.

It will be useful to keep our account of violence as morally neutral as possible. This will enable us to keep separate issues apart. One issue concerns whether or not certain acts properly may be characterized as violent. A second and distinct issue is whether such acts are right or wrong. Nothing is gained by blurring the two issues together by definitional fiat.[6]

Rather than try to *define* violence formally, a task that, if it can be accomplished at all, is likely to take up more space than we have available, it may be more useful to provide a rough explication instead. Such an explication will pick out central features of clear cases of violence but fall short of a list of necessary and sufficient conditions for application of the concept.[7]

Typically or paradigmatically, cases of violence involve the intentional use of physical force designed to harm a person or property. Psychological violence also involves intentional abuse directed against a person, but lacks the element of physical force. Perhaps some forms of violence might be unintentional, but we need not worry about borderline cases for now. Sports, to the extent they involve violence at all, most generally involve physical force, or the threat of physical force, so it is upon physical violence, intentionally directed against opponents, that we will concentrate.

This is not to deny that "violence" is sometimes used loosely in the senses discussed earlier. It is to suggest that when violence is equated simply with the use of force, violence is much less controversial than when it is used in the stronger sense, which has just been sketched above. In any case, as we will see, it is important in any context in which the concept of violence is employed to be clear just which conception of violence is at stake. Perhaps the most controversial use of violence in sports is in boxing. Should boxing be prohibited precisely because it is violent by its very nature?

## BOXING AND ITS CRITICS

What is the case against boxing? Actually, as we will see, there are several kinds of arguments for the view that boxing should be prohibited. A not atypical point of departure for our discussion is the following passage from an editorial in *The New York Times*.

Some people watch boxing to see skill, others just for the blood. Far worse than the blood is the unseen damage. Retinas are dislodged, kidneys bruised and, after repeated pounding, the cerebral cortex accumulates damage to the higher functions of the brain, leading to loss of memory, shambling walk: the traits of the punch-drunk boxer. Can a civilized society plausibly justify the pleasure it may gain from such a sport?[8]

This passage suggests at least two sorts of reasons for prohibiting boxing. The first concerns protection of the boxers themselves. The violence in boxing is just too dangerous to the participants. Therefore, society must protect boxers from potentially serious injury by eliminating the sport of boxing itself. The passage also suggests a second line of argument. The reference to a "civilized society" implies that boxing may have social effects, broader than simply consequences for boxers, that may be harmful to all of us. Let us consider each line of argument in turn.

### Boxing and Paternalism

There is little question that boxing can be harmful to participants. Every boxer who enters the ring faces the possibility of death or serious injury. What can be more plausible then that boxing should be banned to protect the boxers from serious harm and even loss of life?

However, before we accept this argument too quickly, we should consider the following case. Suppose you enjoy playing basketball. Friends, concerned for your welfare, point out that the risk of serious injury in basketball is higher than in such sports as golf or croquet. Therefore, your friends tell you, if you continue to try to play basketball, they will prevent you from doing so, for your own good of course.

The issue at stake here is that of *paternalism*. Roughly stated, paternalism refers to interference with the liberty of agents for what is believed to be their own good. Laws which require motorists to wear seat belts for their own benefit are good examples of paternalistic legislation. An individual's attempt to stop a friend's attempted suicide often will reflect paternalistic motivation at the personal level. Our example of your friends' interference with your basketball playing is yet another illustration.

What makes paternalistic interference problematic? Why shouldn't we interfere with individuals when we believe such action will be of benefit to them? The problem, of course, is individual liberty and autonomy. If we are to respect the liberty and autonomy of persons, how can we interfere with them against their wishes, however benevolent our motives?

Is paternalistic interference ever justified? Perhaps the case against paternalism was formulated best by the British philosopher, John Stuart Mill (1806–1873), in his eloquent defense of personal freedom, *On Liberty*. Mill claimed to be a utilitarian, committed to the view that the sole criterion of right and wrong was production of social utility. At first glance, utilitarianism would seem to allow interference with individual liberty whenever such action produced more social benefits than any available alternative. Interference would be warranted, it would seem, whenever it produced the best consequences obtainable. On this view, consistent utilitarians should be interfering busybodies on the individual level and benevolent but authoritarian versions of Big Brother at the level of the state.

In *On Liberty*, however, Mill advanced important arguments against applying utilitarianism so crudely. Although it is arguable that even Mill was not able to remain within a purely utilitarian ethic, perhaps because conflicts between utility and liberty are unavoidable, he did advance important antipaternalistic arguments based on respect for personal freedom and autonomy.

### The Harm Principle

In one of the most widely discussed passages of *On Liberty*, Mill declared that

> the sole end for which mankind are warranted individually or collectively in interfering with the liberty of action of any of their number is self protection. That the only purpose for which power can be rightfully exercised over any member of a civilized community, against his will, is to prevent harm to others. His own good, either physical or mental, is not a sufficient warrant.[9]

In this passage, Mill distinguishes between *self-regarding* acts, which harm or may harm only the individual performing them, and *other-regarding* acts, which harm or may harm others. According to Mill, the individual's life is his or her business. So long as a person's acts do not harm or threaten others, no interference with them is justified. The only justification for interference with personal liberty is to prevent harm to others.

Clearly, if we adopt the Harm Principle, interference with the liberty of competent adults on paternalistic grounds will be unjustified. Concern for the good of others will not entitle us to interfere with their liberty. This has immediate application to boxing. As sportswriter Pete Axthelm asks, "Do those of us who are well paid to cover fights—or well educated enough to choose not to watch them—have the right to cut off the career choices of the unschooled kids who have traditionally used the ring as a step up out of hopelessness and poverty?"[10]

Accordingly, if we accept the Harm Principle, we have at least a presumptive case against paternalistic interference with boxing. But should we adopt the Harm Principle?

The Principle itself can be defended on a variety of grounds. One can argue, as did Mill at times, that each individual knows his or her interests best and that therefore interference is likely to do more harm than good. The state, or even benevolent friends, cannot know your interests as well as you do and hence are all too likely to interfere at the wrong place and the wrong time for the wrong reasons.

Mill may have overstated this point. Many philosophers have argued that we are not always the best judges of our own interests.[11] However, even if this point is conceded to Mill, it doesn't follow that we are the best judges of *the means* to attain our interests. Thus, if you think it is in your interest to practice your music all day, while I think you should get some healthy exercise, then perhaps there is a sense in which you and not I are the best judge of what is in your interest. But if you think the best way to become a great musician is to watch soap operas all day while I think you should practice your music, it is evident that I know what is in your interest better than you do.

Even if we assume, then, that you are the best judge of your own interests, we still will need to distinguish between two separate questions: (1) What are our interests? and (2) What is the most efficient means for securing our interests? Mill may have been right to warn us that benevolent outsiders are usually less likely than ourselves to know the answer to (1). But even if this point is conceded, his argument does not preclude paternalistic interference designed to promote attainment of goals we ourselves have freely chosen. Others might be in a better position than we are to answer (2).

Thus, *if* what boxers really want is a long and healthy life, and boxing is a threat to health and longevity, paternalistic interference with boxers might be justified as a means of securing for them the goals which they themselves really are after. On the other hand, if boxers really want fame and fortune, rather than health and long life, Mill's argument does count against paternalistic interference with boxing.

Perhaps the Harm Principle would provide a stronger barrier against paternalism if we attempted to justify it, not on grounds that paternalism is likely to be inefficient, but rather on the independent moral grounds that paternalism violates our status as autonomous moral agents. Thus, Mill warned us, we should not construe utility too narrowly, simply in terms of preference satisfaction or frustration. Even if paternalistic interference will make us happier in a narrow sense, by more efficiently getting us what we really want, constant interference with our liberty will stunt our growth and make us incapable of thinking for ourselves. Thus, Mill maintains that

> the human faculties of perception, judgment, discrimination, feeling, mental activity and even moral preference are exercised only in making a choice. . . . The mental and the moral, like the muscular powers, are improved only by being used. . . . He who lets the world . . . choose his plan of life for him, has no need of any other faculty than the ape-like one of imitation.[12]

Mill seems not to be presenting a straightforward utilitarian argument here. Rather, he is appealing to an *ideal* of human development namely; that of the autonomous person. His argument will appeal to anyone who espouses that ideal.

Finally, and perhaps most importantly, one can argue that paternalistic interference with liberty violates human *rights* to personal freedom. While the ground of fundamental human rights is often difficult to explicate, virtually all lists of such rights include human freedom as basic.[13] It surely is plausible to think that if we are the kinds of beings who have rights to anything at all, the right to control our own life must be primary. If our status as purposive, choosing agents is of moral significance, it ought to be respected. Paternalism, by treating us as if we were children, who must be cared for by others, reduces us in moral stature by denying us dignity and respect. Accordingly, if a line of argument such as this can be fleshed out and developed, the Harm Principle can be defended as a corollary of the human right to freedom and autonomy.

### Exceptions to the Harm Principle

But while much can be said in favor of the Harm Principle, even those who defend it acknowledge that it has limitations; limitations set by conflicting principles which also command rational assent.

For example, in *On Liberty,* Mill points out that "this doctrine (the Harm Principle) is meant to apply only to human beings in the maturity of their faculties."[14] Thus, children and the mentally defective are not covered by the Harm Principle. This is surely plausible since the kinds of justification discussed above do not apply fully to such persons; they are not in a position to know their interests better than those of others and they are not (yet) capable of rational, autonomous decision making.

However, while such a limitation on the Harm Principle is acceptable, even to its proponents, it is unclear how it applies to boxing. Clearly, top professional boxers or Olympic class athletes are not children nor do they seem deficient in basic rationality. (If you are tempted to assert that boxers must be irrational to risk serious injury for fame and fortune, you should be prepared to *argue* that you are not expressing a mere preference or prejudice in favor of your own personal values.) They, at least, do not fall under the exception we are considering.

However, children and young adults, such as Louis and Benjii, also participate in boxing. Even if mature, competent adults should be allowed to make their own choices in life, can the same be said of the young? Might not paternalistic restrictions on boxing designed to protect children be justified?

A great deal hangs on what kind of restrictions are at stake and who is to impose them. The question of children's rights raises many complex questions which cannot be addressed here. But one issue worth pursuing concerns whether parents should have absolute rights to decide over the activities in which their children may participate. While many of us, particularly those of us who are parents, may find it natural to sympathize with advocates of absolute parental authority, a strong case can be made that such authority does have limits.

Thus, it is debatable whether parents have the right to refuse to allow life-saving corrective heart surgery for their newborn baby, simply because their baby is a girl and they wanted a boy instead. More to the point, it is unclear that parents may forbid their children to participate in all risky but beneficial activities. After all, all activities, including going to school or crossing a street, contain some element of risk. Can a parent forbid a child to participate in any sport, even golf or jogging, because of the risks involved? If the child is normal and healthy, there is at least some temptation to argue for the child's right to participate in sports, even against parental wishes to the contrary.

But if parents do not have a general right to govern the life of their children, boxing may be a special case because of the special dangers involved. Children may not be sufficiently mature to appreciate the risks involved. (Indeed, we may want to speak of the child's right to protection against overzealous parents who push too hard for participation in risky activities, perhaps unconsciously to promote their own glory rather than to benefit their offspring.)

It is normally better to allow parents to make decisions about their children than to bring in impersonal state agencies, which may be ignorant of special features of the case at hand. Interference in such circumstances, as Mill argued, is likely to be at the wrong place at the wrong time and often will not promote the best interests of those involved.

Inefficiency aside, a state that was permitted to constantly interfere with family life, even for benevolent purposes, would be a clear threat to the liberty and autonomy of its citizens. While a case can be made that children have a right to be protected against cruel or simply misguided parents, if we felt that most parents normally were cruel or seriously misguided, we should work for the elimination of the institution of the family itself, rather than merely interfere in a hit-and-miss fashion.

Perhaps what is needed here is a *presumptive* principle. The presumption is that parents should make important decisions for their children. Presumably, the strength of the parents' rights in this area grows weaker as the child grows older and more mature. The presumption can be overridden by the state in extreme circumstances, such as the case of a parent forbidding life-saving surgery or imposing totally unreasonable and harmful restrictions on a child's life. But the burden of proof would be on the state to show that the normal presumption against interference is outweighed in the particular case at hand.

What are the implications of this discussion for paternalism in boxing? Our discussion suggests that parents may well refuse to allow their children to participate, and indeed surely have a responsibility to seriously consider the pros and cons before giving consent to box. Parental refusal to consent would not by itself constitute an abnormally restrictive or harmful infringement on the child's liberties. On the other hand, it is unclear whether boxing ought to be singled out. Participation in a great many sports, including football and baseball, involves risk of serious injury. So, while participation in boxing may entail special risks, the risks may not be sufficiently great to allow the state to override the assumption of parental decision making in this area.

To summarize, on the view developed here, the state would have the right to override parental consent to participate in a boxing program only under certain conditions. There would have to be clear evidence that boxing is unusually likely to promote serious physical harm, that there is no compensating benefit and that the parents are in effect behaving negligently toward their children. (The state's case would be even stronger if it turned out that the parents were ignorant of the dangers involved.) However, the burden of proof clearly would be on the state. Otherwise, we would be setting a precedent for state agencies to determine what activities our children may or may not participate in and what risks they may be exposed to in almost all areas of life.

On the other hand, the state is not absolved of all responsibility. Surely it has the minimal obligation to inform citizens of unusual dangers involved in a sport. In addition, the state should insure that sports programs in state institutions, such as schools, meet reasonable safety standards. Arguably, the state may set legislative safety standards that commercial instructional and competitive programs must meet, particularly if it is difficult or impossible for parents to monitor such activities directly. What the state cannot do, however, is interfere in the parent-child relationship without especially weighty reasons in its favor. The presumption is that the state should keep out of the private lives of its citizens.

A second kind of exception to the Harm Principle may have a more extensive application to boxing. Perhaps paternalism is acceptable when its goal is not simply to benefit the persons being interfered with but to safeguard their status as rational autonomous agents.[15] For example, suppose a friend, of sound mind and body, is about to take a drug which, while causing pleasurable experiences, is addictive and will eventually destroy her capacity to reason. Aren't you justified in removing her supply of the drug, even against her will? After all, your goal is not to impose your idea of happiness on her. Rather, you are trying to preserve those features that make her an agent capable of choosing her own conception of happiness. Since the very point of the Harm Principle is to protect our status as choosing agents, how can it consistently prohibit the preservation of that status?

A related kind of exception may arise because many of our decisions are not always made thoughtfully. We may decide to do X but, if we were to rationally and impartially consider the situation, we would do Y instead. For example, we may decide not to buckle our seat belts either because we falsely believe that they make no contribution to our safety or because we never formed the habit of using seat belts and simply forget to employ them. Yet, it might still be the case that *if* we were to rationally consider the matter in light of the facts, not only would we decide to buckle the seat belts but we might also prefer that some outside coercive agency, such as the state, require us to use seat belts rather than leave us on our own. Leaving us on our own, in such a case, would not be to respect our rationality and autonomy; it would only be to allow us to endanger ourselves through ignorance or laziness. Legislation, backed by sanctions, might cause us to form the safety habits we would prefer to have but would never otherwise develop.

Accordingly, free and rational agents might allow exceptions to the Harm Principle if such exceptions either (1) are necessary to preserve rationality and autonomy itself, or (2) would be endorsed by rational autonomous agents who were aware of all the relevant facts. How would such a revised Harm Principle apply to boxing?

First, opponents of boxing might argue that typical injuries suffered by fighters do endanger their rational capacities. The constant pounding caused by blows to the head may eventually produce the typical behavior of the "punch-drunk" boxer: slurred speech, imbalance, and impaired reasoning. These behaviors actually are symptoms of underlying and irreversible brain damage. While such injuries are not the inevitable result of participation in boxing, they are frequent enough to justify paternalistic intervention.[16]

Second, rational individuals might well choose to protect themselves against such injury by enpowering the state in advance to intervene paternalistically in their behalf. Gerald Dworkin cites the example of Odysseus and the sirens, from Homer's *Odyssey*, to illustrate this point.

> Odysseus commands his men to tie him to the mast and refuse all future orders to be set free, because he knows the power of the Sirens to enchant men with their songs. Here we are on relatively sound ground in later refusing Odysseus's request to be set free. He may even claim to have changed his mind but since it is *just* such changes that he wishes to guard against, we are entitled to ignore them.[17]

Perhaps a parallel to the case of Odysseus can be drawn if one considers that many professional boxers use the sport as a means of escaping from dire poverty and the ghetto. Is such a "choice" really rational and free, or is it forced by intolerable and unjustly imposed social disadvantage? Free and rational agents might agree that if boxing was permitted as an escape route from social and economic disadvantage, in reality many youngsters would have no choice but to pursue it in order to avoid an unacceptable alternative. Therefore, since the "choice" in question is no more free than the decisions of unprotected Greek sailors to seek the Sirens, it is not covered by the Harm Principle. According to this argument, just as Odysseus consented to being made unfree to follow his future irrational desires, so rational autonomous agents, in possession of all relevant facts, would agree that in our society at least, boxing ought not to be employed as an escape route for the disadvantaged, regardless of what the participants themselves might irrationally desire. After all, they themselves would accept such a conclusion if they could view the situation from a perspective of disinterested freedom and rationality.

However, while such arguments for paternalism are not without force, they hardly seem decisive either. First, consider the claim that we can prevent persons from participating in boxing in order to preserve their status as rational agents. While it is true that boxers run an unusual risk of suffering brain damage, the rewards they hope to gain by running the risk are great. What allows third parties to decide for them that such risks are not worth running? While some observers might not accept such risks themselves, it is far from clear that running a significant risk for a substantial gain is irrational. Moreover, the risk to one's status as an agent is probably not significantly greater than that run by football players, mountain climbers, motorcycle racers, or "workaholics" in business or academia who court heart attacks in the pursuit of professional achievement. If Mill's antipaternalistic arguments work, they justify agents risking their very lives for goals that seem worthwhile to them. Why shouldn't individuals have the right to risk their standing as moral agents or even their own lives if they decide for themselves that the possible gains are worth the risks? After all, it is their own lives and not that of others that they place in jeopardy.

### Paternalism and Free Choice

But do individuals really choose to enter boxing freely and autonomously? Many start boxing as children before the age of consent. Moreover, many boxers enter the sport to escape from poverty and the socioeconomic disadvantages of the ghetto, many of which have been unjustly imposed through racial discrimination. Do such individuals exercise their freedom in deciding to box? Or are they forced into danger by social inequities? If the latter, does the Harm Principle really apply. The boxer's "choice" would be no more an expression of freedom than would Odysseus's surrender to the Sirens. In each case, what looks like a free choice would in reality be a reaction to coercive external pressure. On this view, the athlete is not responding to an offer, i.e. "You can better yourself by becoming a boxer," but rather is reacting to a threat, i.e. "If you don't become a boxer, you will continue to be a victim of social injustice and neglect."

The strategy here is clear. Antipaternalistic arguments based on the Harm Principle are held to be inapplicable to boxing since the Harm Principle only protects the actions of free and autonomous agents. But if boxers are not free and autonomous agents, the Harm Principle cannot be cited against paternalistic interference with their actions. Is such a strategy successful?

Suppose many boxers are forced into the sport because their only alternative is to accept the social disadvantage and injustice into which they were born? Even if true, this point does not justify a broad prohibition of boxing. Rather, it at most supports *eligibility limitations* on who may become a boxer. For example, we may stipulate that no one may become a boxer unless he has some other acceptable alternative career. If such a restriction were adopted, boxing would still exist as a sport. It would be closed only to those who see it as a last resort and who may be "forced" into it by social and economic pressures.

However, even such a limited eligibility restriction may be unjustified. Would we also close other risky sports, such as football and auto racing, to the poor and to victims of injustice? Would risky professions, such as coal mining, also be forbidden? Isn't it condescending to say that the disadvantaged cannot freely and autonomously evaluate the risks for themselves?

In our society, where the alternative to a career in boxing is likely to be not starvation, but a more mundane job or receipt of welfare, it does seem plausible to view boxing as an opportunity rather than a threat. A career as a boxer is not the only minimally acceptable choice available. Rather, it may constitute the only available route to fame, fortune, and a chance to achieve excellence in a career.

What is exploitative, and what will be considered later under the heading of exploitation of the black athlete, is to present sports as a major escape route from the effects of poverty and discrimination. In reality, only an infinitesimal percentage of those who try to achieve professional success in sports ever actually attain it. But many of those who try, and who are doomed to failure, neglect to develop other skills, or acquire the educational background, which would insure a long and productive career outside of athletics. Perhaps the greatest harm caused by the myth that sports promotes upward mobility is the "opportunity cost" it inflicts on many disadvantaged young athletes; the hours which might productively be devoted to study are spent in gyms, on fields, and in boxing rings instead.

Those involved professionally in sports, particularly coaches, have a responsibility to acquaint young athletes with the realities of the odds of success in professional sports. On the other hand, it cannot be denied that athletics can sometimes lead to external goods which would not otherwise be available. Thus, if individuals are to be treated as free and autonomous persons, it is up to them to make the ultimate choice of which path to follow. Parents, teachers, and coaches have obligations to prepare their children, students, and players for what they may face in the future, but as the age of maturity is reached, individuals can no longer be forced to follow a road that, whatever others think, they themselves no longer regard as the best one to travel.

We can conclude, then, that while paternalistic arguments in favor of a prohibition on boxing are not totally without force, they are not conclusive either. On the contrary, our concern for individual liberty and autonomy justifies us in placing the burden of proof on the paternalist. Although further discussion might yield a different result, it appears that the burden has not yet been met where boxing and other risky sports are at issue.

### Does Boxing Harm Society?

So far, we have been assuming that the only issue at stake concerning boxing is paternalism. But what if boxing is not simply self-regarding but has effects on others? If so, boxing would not be protected by the Harm Principle. The Harm Principle forbids interference with self-regarding action, but permits interference with other-regarding action in order to prevent harm to third parties.

But how can boxing harm others? On the surface, at least, it looks as if the only ones who will be harmed are the boxers themselves.

However, appearances can be deceiving. To see how boxing might harm society, consider an imaginary sport of Mayhem. The rules of Mayhem are simple. Twenty volunteers are placed in a ring with swords, after being divided into teams. The players on the winning, i.e. surviving, team each get $1,000,000. Does it follow that if paternalistic interference with Mayhem is unwarranted, there are no other reasons for prohibiting it?[18] Isn't it plausible to think that although no spectators are directly harmed—the gladiators do not use their swords on fans, even on those who boo—indirect harm is substantial? Children may come to idolize trained killers. (Would kids collect "gladiator bubblegum cards" with kill ratio statistics on the back side?) Violence would be glorified. The value of human life almost inevitably would be cheapened. Killing might come to be viewed as a sport to be carried out with skill and élan. While such effects might not be inevitable, their likelihood is sufficient to justify a civilized society in banning Mayhem for reasons which have nothing to do with paternalism.

Can't a similar argument be applied to boxing? As *The New York Times* argues in an editorial, "the public celebration of violence cannot be a private matter."[19]

On this view, boxing, like Mayhem, teaches our children the wrong values, glorifies the destruction of our fellows, and rewards those who would intentionally hurt opponents. Although many sports involve bodily contact and the use of physical force against opponents, only in boxing do the competitors *intend* to hurt one another. Arguably, boxing is violent, not just in the weak sense of involving physical force but in the strong sense in which competitors have as their goal the infliction of injury upon an opponent. Do we want our society to glorify such an activity under the name of sport?

Remarks such as the above make implicit appeal to *two* separate and distinct kinds of arguments. One kind is causal in character. According to this argument, public celebration of the violent sport of boxing *causes* others to be influenced by example and become more violent, or more tolerant of violence, themselves. In this way, the sport of boxing, insofar as it is public and institutionalized, raises the overall level of violence in society. According to the second kind of argument, regardless of the causal effects of boxing, we ought not to shed fame and fortune on the violent. Just as it is wrong to applaud a murder, so too is it wrong to applaud violence in the ring. Violence should not be publicly celebrated.

The first argument needs to be supported by empirical evidence that in fact may be difficult to obtain. However, many psychologists have maintained for some time that we can be influenced by models, and that if society presents violent persons as its heroes, whether on television, in the movies, or in the ring, this is bound to have subtle but significant effects upon behavior.[20] While much hangs on the empirical evidence, there are conceptual and moral points at stake that it would be dangerous to ignore.

For the psychological argument based on the power of modeling to go through, boxing must be a genuine example or model of violence. Perhaps many spectators take it as such. Surely, the presentation of boxing in the media emphasizes the violent side of the sport. But is this the way spectators *must* see boxing? Isn't it just as plausible to view boxing as an example of *controlled aggression*, limited by rules? Surely, it is not essential to the sport of boxing that it be viewed as violent. Instead, the skill, power, grace, and courage of the contestants can be admired, as well as the commitment of the boxers to stay within the framework of the sport and the norms that govern it. Conceived as such, why isn't boxing an example of the human ability to control and deal with violence rather than a glorification of it? Even if boxing in our own society falls more under the latter heading than the former one, perhaps the proper reaction is not to prohibit boxing but to change the way we perceive and publicly present it.

However, even if this point is mistaken and boxing is a clear example of violence in sport, one which does have a causal effect on others, it does not *follow* that boxing ought to be prohibited. The "simple" inference that since boxing can effect others for the worse, it is fair game for legislative prohibition actually raises a host of complicated issues.

Perhaps most important, the notion of other-regarding behavior arguably is being construed too broadly. After all, if I read a book in the privacy of my own home, its argument could change my views in ways that may harm others. For example, suppose I read a book advocating an undisciplined kind of secondary education where students study only what makes them feel good. As a result of my reading, I become a proponent of that position and am instrumental in securing its implementation in local schools. *If* such a view is educationally harmful, my reading of the book might result in harm to students, as well as to future citizens who may be exposed to such untrained graduates of the public schools. The trouble with construing other-regarding action so broadly, then, is that almost all action, including that of reading controversial books in the privacy of one's own home, would fall under such a heading. The sphere of liberty would be reduced to almost nothing.

As Mill himself may have suggested, the place to interfere with behavior is where it *directly* impinges on others.[21] Surely, some indirect danger to others must be tolerated as the price of allowing individuals a significant degree of personal freedom. Boxing might set a public example which causes a good deal of harm. Are we justified in interfering with the liberty of the boxers and fans in order to prevent such harm? Surely the time to interfere is when the spectator breaks the law and not with boxing itself.

Such a conclusion should not be accepted too quickly, however. If spectators at boxing matches were transformed into "clear and present dangers" to their fellow citizens, so that murders, rapes, and muggings were carried out by spectators soon after leaving the arena, a plausible case for interference with boxing surely would exist. But that hardly seems to be the case. Perhaps what we should conclude is that the burden of proof is on proponents of interference to show that they are not unduly sacrificing liberty for minimal gains in the prevention of social harm.

The second kind of argument to be considered maintains that it simply is wrong to celebrate violence. This argument does not rest on controversial empirical claims about the effect boxing has on society. Its point is that since it is wrong to intentionally use physical force to inflict harm on others, it is also wrong to celebrate the intentional infliction of harm on others. Such celebration is wrong, not because of its consequences, but because of what it is.[22]

We might respond by appealing once again to the personal freedom of boxers and fans. But while, as we have seen, such arguments have considerable force, opponents might argue that the appeal to liberty is not always decisive. Although freedom has great value, they might question whether it always should override all other competing values. Do we really want to say, for example, that in the name of freedom, the personal liberty of "players" to participate in Mayhem should be inviolate? After all, interference with Mayhem restricts freedom as much as interference with my private reading habits.

Thus, we might want to follow British moralist Lord Devlin in arguing that for a society to be viable, a minimal public morality which serves as the glue binding different factions together must exist.[23] Surely, civility is part of that glue. Yet the celebration of violence undermines that glue by calling into question that minimal civility without which society breaks down.

Lord Devlin's position might imply, then, that if boxing is essentially violent, if the intention to injure opponents is essential to boxing, the appeal to liberty may be an insufficient defense to boxing's critics. Liberty, on such a view, may justifiably be curtailed when a direct threat to the public order begins. However, if we accept such a view, we would seem to make liberty hostage to often indefensible interpretations of what constitutes or threatens the public order.

## Boxing and the Ethics of Competition

Our discussion seems to have left us between a rock and a hard place. If we take a hard line and refuse to limit individual liberty, we can defend the practice of boxing just as it is. But if we take such a hard libertarian line, would we have any grounds left for prohibiting Mayhem, let alone local gang wars, so long as none of the participants have been forced to take part? On the other hand, if we prohibit boxing as well as Mayhem on other regarding grounds, or in defense of a minimal public morality which holds society together, what activity is likely to remain immune from external interference?

Perhaps the dilemma can be avoided, or at least blunted, if the underlying assumption that boxing is essentially violent can be called into question. According to a widely held view, boxing is a special case in sport; only boxers, in virtue of the nature of their sport, aim at injuring opponents. Injuries happen in other sports, but only boxing requires that its participants win precisely by harming the opposition.

In Chapter Two, it was suggested that competition in sport should be conceived of as the mutual quest for challenge among competitors. It is as if each competitor has contracted to do his or her best so as to stimulate the others to do their best. What follows if we apply this model to boxing?

The most direct implication is that boxers should intend not to injure competitors but rather to box skillfully so as do their best and bring out the best in their opponents. Perhaps contemporary professional boxing encourages the formation of intentions to do violence. However, it was at one time true that the goal of fencers was to skewer their enemies. Fencers today need not have any such desire. Why can't the same be true of a reformed sport of boxing?

If boxing is conceived of as a sport, its goal should be demonstration of certain martial skills, not the injuring of rival competitors. Proponents of boxing as a sport surely would argue that in boxing at its best, it is the skill of the athletes and not the scent of blood that would be of interest. Of course, particular boxers may want to harm their opponents, just as a particular pitcher may want to bean a particular batter, but it is hard to see why such intentions *must* be part of boxing any more than they must be part of baseball or any other sport.

Accordingly, as was argued earlier, boxing can be seen as a paradigm of the controlled use of force rather than as socially acceptable violence. Boxers, on such a view, should use force to demonstrate their skills and bring out those of competitors, not to intentionally injure opponents.

In addition, modifications which channel boxing in the direction of fencing and away from Mayhem should be adopted. The nature of the reforms undoubtedly will be controversial, but they surely must include the introduction of safer equipment, more stringent medical monitoring of fighters, greater emphasis on scoring rather than on knockouts, and perhaps the penalizing of punches to the head. While boxing will never be as sedate as modern fencing, it can be modified so as to more clearly distinguish it from Mayhem.

Of course, hard-nosed libertarians may be quite right to argue that *the state* has no business interfering even with boxing at its most violent on the grounds that liberty of consenting adults is inviolate. But even if this point is correct, which is controversial, it concerns only the permissibility of *legal* prohibition of boxing. It does not follow that boxing at its most violent is an *ethically* defensible sport. It is when athletic competition treats competitors as persons, by application of the model of the mutual quest for excellence, that it is ethically defensible.

Defenders of boxing might object that such sanitization of boxing removes those very qualities which make it such a fascinating sport. The opportunity to show courage, to do one's best in the face of pain, and to demonstrate skill in the use of brute power would all be lost if boxing were made more like fencing. On such a view, the loss would not be worth the gain.

This point merits serious consideration. But before it is accepted, we ought to ask whether the same argument could be made in behalf of Mayhem. If this defense of boxing is accepted, aren't we also committed by application of the ethical requirement of systematic consistency (see Chapter One) to the view that society must allow gladiatorial contests, lest liberty be violated? Surely sports such as baseball, basketball, and soccer give ample opportunities for the demonstration of courage, the capacity to overcome injury and use force skillfully without essentially involving the intent to inflict injury upon an opponent.

Finally, a proponent of boxing may deny a key premise of the critics; the claim that boxers intentionally aim at injuring their opponents. "Boxers do aim at boxing skillfully," a proponent may maintain, "but it just so happens that a skillful punch often results in the unintentional infliction of injury."

Superficially, this claim resembles the suggestion that a football player who injures an opponent by throwing a clean block may not have intended to inflict harm. In such a case, the player may have wanted only to open a hole for the ball carrier. By doing so, he unintentionally inflicts an injury on a defender. But is this really analogous to the situation in boxing or is it different? After all, in boxing, the quickest way to win is through a knockout. Alternately, one can win by injuring an opponent so severely that although conscious, he cannot continue the bout. Unfortunately, the attempt to distinguish between the act of hitting and the unintended consequence of injuring an opponent seems suspiciously like the attempt to distinguish between pulling the trigger of a loaded gun one has aimed at an enemy and the victim's death. Where the effect is so closely linked to the action, the burden of proof surely does fall on those who want to distinguish the attempt to knock out an opponent from the attempt to injure him.

Our discussion suggests, then, that even if boxing should be immune from legal interference or prohibition on libertarian grounds, radical reform of the sport is morally warranted. Emphasis should be on scoring and fistic skill, not on infliction of injury. *Perhaps* society has no right to force boxers to give up their sport or prevent spectators from watching bouts. (Does it have the right to prohibit gladiatorial contests?) But ethical concerns about the nature of good sport put the burden of proof on proponents of boxing to show why significant reforms should not be adopted.

## VIOLENCE AND CONTACT SPORTS

Can arguments concerning violence in boxing be carried over to discussions of other contact sports? For example, if it can be successfully argued that boxing should be reformed or even prohibited because of the violence it involves, why can't the same be said of football as well?

Critics of football maintain that football is a violent sport. Coaches and fans urge players to "smash," "smear" or "bury" the opposition. Players are viewed as pieces of meat to be expended on neutralizing the warriors of the other side. On this view, football is a miniaturized version of war. All too often the intent of the participants and spectators is to win by any means possible, including the inflicting of injury on the other side. When a coach declares on national television that "anytime you get a chance to take 'em out . . . I expect and encourage you to do it," the chances are that the values being expressed are not isolated within the profession.[24]

Even players who claim to stay within the rules admit that physical intimidation of opponents is a key part of their game. As Oakland Raider free safety Jack Tatum puts it in his, some would say aptly named, book *They Call Me Assassin*, "My idea of a good hit is when the victim wakes up on the sidelines with the train whistles blowing in his head and wondering who he is and what ran over him."[25] Unfortunately, one of Tatum's hits in a game against the New England Patriots resulted in what appears to be the permanent paralysis of the Patriot's pass receiver, Darryl Stingley.

Tatum claims that although he hits hard, he plays within the rules and does not take illegal "shots" at opponents. On his view, he is paid to make sure pass receivers don't make catches in his territory. A good way to achieve this goal is to let them know they will get hit hard when running pass patterns in his area. Then, the next time a pass is thrown to them, they may think too much about what is about to hit them and concentrate less on making the catch. As Tatum puts it, "do I let the receiver have the edge and give him the chance to make catches around me because I'm a sensitive guy or do I do what I am paid to do?"[26]

It is understandable, then, why to its many critics, football is a sport which glorifies violence, encourages militaristic attitudes, and amounts to a public celebration of many of our worst values. In effect, these critics hold that football, particularly big-time college and professional football, are to contemporary American society what gladiatorial contests were to the Romans.

Paul Hoch, author of *Rip Off the Big Game*, a highly ideological critique of American sport but one which raises many serious issues for consideration, sees football as an expression of suppressed violence in the American psyche. Thus, he suggests that because violence is rule-governed in football, as opposed to the random violence of racial disorders or radical political protests, it "provides powerful ideological support for the official-ized, rule-governed violence in society, in which judges have the final say. In short, the fans are supposed to identify with the distorted framework of law and order, both on the football field and in society, irrespective of what that law and order is supposed to protect."[27]

Unfortunately, an atmosphere of violence pervades a good deal of big-time American sport, with football perhaps constituting a paradigm example. Thus, Hoch maintains,

> if the fans can be encouraged . . . to demand higher and higher levels of glad-iatorial violence, sports owners can easily supply it. Professional athletes are encouraged to maim one another, not only by the macho-minded sports writers and fans . . . but by the knowledge that if they're not tough enough there are literally thousands . . . of players around to take their jobs. . . . In a militarized society, gladiatorial combat brings in profits at the box office. So its all part of the game. But whose game?[28]

In a similar vein, James Michener reports on brutality in some college football programs. In one case, smaller players on a university team "were forced to wrestle huge linemen under the chicken wire, and the losers had to keep wrestling until they won, always screaming and cursing and trying to draw blood like some kind of animals."[29]

### The Ethics of Violence in Football

The charges discussed above can be reduced to two major claims. First, football is held to be a violent sport. Second, because of its emphasis on disciplined violence within the rules, football encourages fan acceptance of official violence while discouraging external criticism of the rules themselves. In other words, football is not ideologically neutral, at least in our society. It encourages a positive attitude towards officially sanctioned violence and discourages social criticism and the use of violence for social change.

Many of the distinctions which arose in our discussion of boxing also apply to analysis of the charges against football. In particular, it is important to distinguish between violence that is *intrinsic* and violence that is *extrinsic* to football, and secondly, it is important to distinguish between violence and the use of force.

Surely, violence, in the sense of the use of force intended to harm an opponent, normally is indefensible in sport. With the possible exception of such sports as boxing, players have not consented to become targets of violence and there is little reason to think it would be rational for them to do so. From the high school player, who wants to keep a healthy body so he can participate in sports throughout a lifetime, to the pro star whose career and earnings can be cut short by a serious injury, players have a clear interest in keeping violence (as opposed to legitimate body contact) out of football. In the long run, so do coaches, since their own stars are just as vulnerable as the stars on opposing teams. Spectators would lose, too, if exciting players spent more time on crutches than on the field because of intentionally administered injuries.

In any case, violence directed by players against players is no more ethically defensible than violence directed against persons in other contexts. Violence directed against an opponent treats that person as a mere means or thing to be used for the gratification or advancement of the agent. It violates the ethic of competition, which requires that opponents be conceived of as partners in a mutual quest for excellence, as well as the deeper underlying moral requirement of respect for persons.

But is violence in the strong sense of the use of force intended to harm another really intrinsic to football? Is football essentially a violent game or is violence a *misuse* of force within the sport?

Football clearly is a contact sport which requires the use of bodily force. It does not follow, however, that football is intrinsically violent. If critics want to argue the opposite, they need to do more than simply point out that football is a contact sport. The most that has been established is that unfortunately violence is frequently part of football, not that football is intrinsically violent. As we have seen, the use of force is morally quite distinct from violence.

But how is the line between violence and the use of force to be drawn? When Jack Tatum attempts to intimidate an opposing receiver through "good hits," then is he being violent? Tatum himself might say that he does not want to injure his opponent but only to make him afraid, and only through moves permitted by the rules. But what is the opposing receiver afraid of if not getting hurt? On the other hand, what if we say Tatum is using violence? Does it follow that the huge linemen who try to physically wear down their opposite numbers through constant application of force are violent too? And if we say they are violent, what part of football isn't violent? Is such violence unethical?

Perhaps it will help if we turn away from football for a moment and consider examples of intimidation in other sports. In baseball, a pitch thrown with the intent of injuring the batter—a "beanball" thrown at the batter's head—clearly constitutes an act of reprehensible violence. No game justifies the attempt to maim or kill an opponent. But what if a batter continually leans over the inside corner of the plate, in an attempt to deprive the pitcher of a portion of the strike zone? If the pitcher throws some inside "brushback" pitches, which are designed not to hit the batter, but to force him to move back to a position which is strategically advantageous to the pitcher, is violence involved? What of the tennis player who sees an opponent charging the net and smashes a return directly at the opposing player, not with the intent to injure, but with the goal of scoring a quick point?

Suppose one thinks that the brushback pitch and the forehand smash at an opponent are permissible moves within sport, and that if they do involve violence at all, they do so in an ethically defensible way. What might an ethical defense of such practices look like? Are there any principles we might discover in formulating such a defense which can be applied to football?

To begin with, we might note that sports often do involve the use of force against opponents to achieve strategic goals. Not infrequently, this use of force will involve the risk of injury. Presumably, participants are willing to take such a risk because they believe the risks are outweighed by the benefits of participation. The key ethical question, it might be claimed, is whether the use of force in question takes unfair advantage of the *vulnerability* of one's opponent. Thus, major league batters are supposed to have the reflexes and ability to avoid brushback pitches. The pitcher is not throwing at a sitting duck. In contrast, a beanball thrown just behind a batter's head takes advantage of the hitter's superb reflexes to inflict injury. The batter sees the pitch is inside, and ducks backward right into the path on which the ball is thrown. On the other hand, a brushback pitch, which might be ethically defensible when thrown in a major league game, would be ethically indefensible if thrown by a big league pitcher against a 50-year-old, out of shape businessman who hasn't played ball in decades.

If these suggestions have force, they support what we might call the Vulnerability Principle, or VP. According to the VP, the use of force against an opponent in sport is ethically indefensible just when the opponent's physical position or condition is such that no effective strategic response is possible and as a result it is highly likely that injury will result.

If we apply the VP to football, we find that the use of force by linemen against one another is acceptable. Physical intimidation of one line by another is permissible if it amounts to wearing down the opposition by the constant infliction of force, so long as the opponents are in a position to respond with strategic countermoves, i.e. blocks, and are not in an unusual position of physical risk. On the other hand, a hit from the blind side by a free safety on a receiver who is not the target of a pass catches the receiver in a position of vulnerability where no effective countermove is possible. Such a blow, therefore, is ethically dubious. Indeed, defensive backs, including Jack Tatum, have suggested that the rules be rewritten so as to provide more protection for receivers. Unfortunately, it may be the belief that a wide-open, high risk game is what brings in the dollars that contributes as much to injuries in big-time football as the moves of the players on the field.

Although our discussion of violence in football has not been conclusive, we have seen that the use of force to deliberately harm an opponent has no place in the sport. If there is a moral difference between such behavior and criminal assault, we have yet to be told what it is. On the other hand, we have seen that it is difficult to draw the line between defensible and indefensible uses of force for strategic purposes. Perhaps the VP represents a first step toward the formulation of a useful principle in this area, although it clearly needs to be examined and reformulated more rigorously in the light of counterexample. In any case, we have seen that violence is not equivalent to the mere use of force. The challenge contact sports provide is in the skilled and controlled use of force for strategic ends, and they are not to be condemned for that alone.

### Is Football Conservative?

What about the charge that football supports values such as deference to the powerful and the legitimacy of officially sanctioned violence? Does football function ideologically to support conservatism and the *status quo?*

In assessing the charge that football serves a conservative function in our society, the first thing to note is the ambiguity of the claim being made. Perhaps it means that the great attention given to big-time football, and to other major sports, *causes* people to tolerate an unjust situation, perhaps by distracting them from their more serious problems or perhaps by inducing them to identify with power, as Hoch suggests. Alternately, perhaps what is being claimed is that the values implicit in the play of football are themselves objectionable; football is warlike or football requires unquestioning acceptance of officially sanctioned violence. Here what we have is not an empirical claim about the effects of football on the American public but rather a moral analysis of the kind of values embedded in the play of the game. Let us examine each kind of claim in turn.

The causal theses, of course, ultimately must be confirmed or disconfirmed by empirical data, not by philosophizing. In fact, the existing data is difficult to interpret but can perhaps be read to provide modest support for the role of sport in reinforcing conventional values.[30] Nevertheless, as interesting as the interpretation of empirical studies might be, we need to keep in mind the philosophical points which interpretation of any studies in this area presuppose.

To begin with, we must remember not to confuse correlation with causality. Suppose empirical studies show that football fans, or even players and coaches, tend to be more tolerant of officially sanctioned violence, less tempted to rock the boat to correct injustice, and more disposed to respect those in power, regardless of what they command, than those not involved with football. Can one conclude on the basis of such data that involvement with football *produces* such a personality? One cannot. For one thing, as we noted in a similar context in Chapter Two, it is entirely possible that people with such traits become football fans and not that football fans become such people. Alternately, some as-yet-unknown third factor might produce both involvement in football and the associated traits.

There is another, perhaps more profound, philosophical issue at stake. If what we are trying to measure are such traits as "unquestioning obedience to authority," "tolerance of injustice," "acceptance of official violence," and "unwillingness to challenge the rules," we need to be careful that we do not beg the question in favor of our own values. What one investigator believes to be blind obedience, another may see as admirable loyalty. In addition, value judgments may be called for in estimating what counts as injustice, what counts as blind or uncritical obedience and what degree of acceptance of authority is normal or justified. Accordingly, although the critics are quite right to raise the question of the social effects of sports and their value, they may smuggle in moral conclusions that have not been adequately defended. For example, they may assume that football is essentially violent, an assumption which we have seen needs explication and defense and which is far from self-evident. Or they may assume that violence is "just part of the game," ignoring the distinction between violence and force.

What of the second thesis, based on moral analysis, that regardless of its causal effects, football expresses by its very nature the values of blind obedience, militarism, toleration of official violence, and fear of going outside the rules to promote change? Does football *express* an ideologically loaded set of conservative values, whether or not it causes others to adopt them?

It will be useful to approach this issue by asking what it *means* to say that football, or any other sport, *expresses* certain values. On one hand, it might mean that action based upon particular values is or ought to be rewarded within the context of the sport. Thus, football would be essentially violent, in this sense, if acts of violence were rewarded within the game. As we have seen, players, coaches, and fans all have strong reasons to support a system of rules prohibiting violence (in the sense of the intentional use of force designed to harm opponents), as well as a system of sanctions supporting such rules. While the temptation to cheat on particular occasions might be overwhelming, all those involved in the sport have incentives to keep such occasions few and far between, and to do their best to make sure isolated acts of violence do not pay off. Clearly, there are grounds for denying that violence *ought* to be rewarded within football and for condemning those who encourage it.

There is a second sense is which a sport can be said to express certain values. In this sense, a sport expresses values just when playing the sport well requires that the players exhibit the values in question. For example, it can be argued that basketball at its best expresses the value of teamwork. Thus, the good basketball coach will teach his players that a coordinated team performance is more valuable than uncoordinated individual achievement. While basketball is often exciting precisely because of the outstanding moves of individual players such as Dr. J., the sport is most pleasing when players employ their individual skills within a framework of team goals.

Does football express violence in the sense that to play well, players must aim at hurting opponents? While some coaches may encourage violent attitudes among their players, and some players may not need much encouragement, such an approach is hardly an essential element of good football. Toughness may be a valuable attribute of football players, but meanness is not. Moreover, while the line between the defensible and indefensible use of force in contact sports is not always easy to draw, principles such as the VP may be used to reform the rules so as to make them more closely conform to moral requirements.

What about the claim that excellence in football requires blind subservience to the coach, and hence expresses the value of uncritical acceptance of the dictates of those in power? What football teaches us, critics such as Hoch tend to assert, is that violence is permissible if it is ordered by those in the power structure. After all, players are expected to carry out orders and "execute" the coach's commands, or those of the quarterback, without question. This is direct opposition to the kind of questioning of those in power that is so necessary for the workings of democracy and the critical inquiry which gives it life.

While there are too many examples of authoritarianism in sport, it may go too far to criticize sport itself rather than those who misuse power within it. In addition, we need to be careful not to beg important questions by viewing sports through our own ideological blinders. Thus, one might argue that football is conservative because it teaches us to follow existing rules, or with equal force argue that it is liberal because it teaches us that authority figures who break the rules are open to moral criticism. After all, the notion that American Presidents are not above the law is hardly an illiberal notion. Surely, there is no more reason to say that a football coach who requires his players to practice hard is teaching "blind subservience to authority" any more than does the philosophy professor who expects students to read assignments.

To conclude, we have not been given reason to believe that football illustrates or expresses indifference to or tolerance of violence. We already have seen that there is reason to doubt that football is essentially violent in the first place. On the contrary, we can plausibly argue that at its best, it illustrates not violence but the controlled use of force. On the other hand, to the extent that the actual practice of football is violent, or involves the indefensible use of force, it is subject to moral criticism. Thus, while violence may often occur in football, its mere presence doesn't teach people to think of it as justified or reasonable.

Of course, owners of pro teams may think that violence sells tickets. The media may too often glorify violence in the attempt to secure a wider audience. But whether we tolerate such abuses in sport depends at least in part on the critical principles we accept and apply in evaluating athletics. If we are ethically required to view competitors as partners in a mutual quest for excellence through challenge, a violent attitude toward them is surely unjustified. The ethic of good sports requires that we distinguish hard but legitimate contact from violence. It is far from clear that football illustrates the value of the latter rather than providing grounds, based on the ethic of good competition, for its condemnation.

### The Ideal and the Actual in Philosophy of Sports

It is understandable that some critics of violence in sports may be impatient with the discussion so far. In their view, the discussion has been an exercise in developing an ideal which has perhaps been too tolerant of actual abuses. "It is all too easy to say that football is not *necessarily* violent," such a critic might argue, "when the important task is to show what is wrong with actual practice and to promote change."

While much of our discussion has been concerned with developing an ideal of good sport, it hardly lacks practical implications. It is difficult to understand how we could even identify abuses in sport unless we had some grasp of what principles were being violated in the first place. In addition, without some standards at which to aim, we would not know the proper direction for moral change.

Of course, moral reform involves far more than efficiently implementing an ideal. At a minimum, the ideal must be implemented in a fair and just way. For example, would it be fair to simply prohibit boxing without making some provision for employment for boxers whose jobs we would be eliminating? It is possible that the moral and practical costs of implementing some reforms might be so high that we are bound to settle for "second best" solutions. Be that as it may, unless we know what principles should apply in sport, how are we to even tell what needs to be corrected in current practice?

### Against Violence in Sports

In this chapter, it has been argued that violence in sport, in the sense of force directed at inflicting harm on others, is incompatible with the ethic of athletic competition as the mutual quest for excellence. Since ethical competitors view each other as cooperating in the posing of challenges, they do not view opponents as obstacles to be gotten out of the way. Rather, they encourage opponents to play their best so that new and better challenges can be faced by all.

While we have rejected the view that football is to be condemned as illegitimately violent, it is important to see that the argument of the chapter counts against many defenders of the "boys will be boys" school of thought as well. For example, those who defend constant fighting in hockey by claiming roughness is "part of the game" make the very same logical error as those who confuse the use of force with violence. While body checking may be a defensible part of hockey, at least insofar as its goal is to advance play rather than to injure opponents, hitting an opponent with a hockey stick with the desire to "take him out" surely is not. If it is, the "game" being played is not a morally defensible one. Similarly, the encouraging of hockey professionals to fight so as to sell more tickets is about on a moral par with the subsidization of Mayhem.

However, we should not confuse the thesis that violence often is a part of sport, and is even exploited for commercial reasons, with the stronger thesis that sports are essentially violent. It is because the latter thesis is so questionable that we have grounds for condemning violence and its exploitation in the name of good sport.

If competition in sport is conceived of as the mutual quest for excellence, which it should be if competitors are to be morally respected as persons, then violence in the strong sense has no place in it. A defensible sport ethic must avoid the twin errors of, on one hand, equating the use of force in sports with indefensible violence and, on the other, tolerating violence because of a mistaken belief that since sport is a kind of competitive war, anything goes as long as it works in the pursuit of victory.

### NOTES

[1]Frank Deford, "An Encounter to Last an Eternity," *Sports Illustrated*, Vol. 58, No. 15 (April 11, 1983), p. 71. All excerpts from this article are reprinted courtesy of *Sports Illustrated*, from the April 11, 1983 issue. © 1983 Time Inc.

[2]Ibid., p. 72.

[3]Ibid., p. 79.

⁴Ibid., p. 81.

⁵Bill Gilbert and Lisa Twyman, "Violence: Out of Hand in the Stands" *Sports Illustrated*, Vol. 58, No. 4 (Jan. 31, 1983) is a brief but good account of problems arising from violence among spectators at sports events.

⁶Useful philosophical discussions of the nature and justification of violence are to be found in Jerome A. Shaffer, ed., *Violence* (New York: David McKay Company, 1971). The blurring of the normative and descriptive in political discourse has been criticized by Felix Oppenheim in his *Political Concepts: A Reconstruction* (Chicago: University of Chicago Press, 1981).

⁷Indeed, many philosophers would deny that an analysis in terms of necessary and sufficient conditions can be given for many expressions in ordinary language.

⁸Editorial, *The New York Times*, Dec. 14, 1982, p. 30. © 1982 by The New York Times Company. Reprinted by permission.

⁹John Stuart Mill, *On Liberty*, (1859), edited by Elizabeth Rapaport (Indianapolis: Hackett Publishing Company, 1978), p. 9.

¹⁰Pete Axthelm, "Don't Count Boxing Out," *Newsweek*, Dec. 20, 1982, p. 60. Copyright 1982 by *Newsweek*, Inc. All rights reserved. Reprinted by permission.

¹¹But suppose, to borrow an example from Bernard Gert, that your overriding goal at present is to cut yourself in little pieces, while you assign lower priority to your desire to see a psychiatrist to rid yourself of your primary desire. Suppose I refuse to hand over a machete to you. Must we accept your reply, "Well, I'm the best judge of my own interest, aren't I?" See Bernard Gert, *The Moral Rules*, (New York: Harper & Row, 1970), p. 30.

¹²Mill, *On Liberty*, p. 56.

¹³For a discussion of the nature and justification of natural or human rights, see Norman E. Bowie and Robert L. Simon, *The Individual and the Political Order* (Englewood Cliffs, N.J.: Prentice-Hall, 1977), Chapter 3, where it is argued that welfare rights as well as liberty rights are fundamental moral entitlements.

¹⁴Mill, *On Liberty*, p. 9.

¹⁵For a defense of such a position, see Gerald Dworkin, *Paternalism*, in Richard A. Wasserstrom, ed., *Morality and the Law* (Belmont, California: Wadsworth, 1971), pp. 107-126.

¹⁶An accessible discussion of the medical evidence on the effects of boxing and some of its implications for policy is found in Robert H. Boyle and Wilmer Ames, "Too Many Punches, Too Little Concern," *Sports Illustrated*, April 11, 1983, pp. 42-67.

¹⁷Dworkin, *Paternalism* pp. 119-120.

¹⁸The Mayhem example is based on a similar illustration used by Irving Kristol in his essay "Pornography, Obscenity and the Case for Censorship," *The New York Times Magazine*, March 28, 1971, reprinted in Joel Feinberg and Hyman Gross, eds., *Philosophy of Law* (Encino: Dickenson Publishing Comany, Inc., 1975), pp. 165-171.

¹⁹Editorial, *The New York Times*, Dec. 14, 1982, p. 30. © 1982 by The New York Times Company. Reprinted by permission.

²⁰For an account of the role of observation and models in learning, see Albert Bandura, *Social Learning Theory* (Englewood Cliffs, N.J.: Prentice-Hall, 1977). For discussion of the contemporary psychology of moral development by philosophers and psychologists, see the symposium on moral development in *Ethics*, Vol. 92., No. 3 (April, 1982).

²¹Mill, *On Liberty*, pp. 78-80.

²²Similarly, it might be argued that even if the glorification of a rape, say in a work of literature, does not tend to cause anyone to commit actual rape, rape is simply not the sort of thing that ought to be glorified, even if only in a work of fiction.

²³See Lord Patrick Devlin, "Morals and the Criminal Law," in Wasserstrom, *Morality and the Law*, pp. 24-48.

²⁴Paul Hoch, *Rip Off the Big Game*, (Garden City, N.Y.: Doubleday & Co., Inc., 1972) p. 27. Copyright © 1972 by Paul Hoch. Reprinted by permission of Doubleday & Company, Inc.

²⁵Jack Tatum with Bill Kushner, *They Call Me Assassin* (New York, Everest House, 1979), p. 12.

[26]Ibid. p. 176.

[27]Hoch, *Rip Off the Big Game,* p. 22.

[28]Ibid., pp. 27–28.

[29]James Michener, *Sports in America* (New York: Random House, 1976), pp. 433–435.

[30]For discussion, see Eldon E. Snyder and Elmer A. Spreitzer, *Social Aspects of Sport* (Englewood Cliffs, N.J.: Prentice-Hall, 1983), pp. 93–96.

# CHAPTER FOUR
# ETHICS
# IN COMPETITION
## Enhancing performance
## through drugs

Competition in sports, it has been argued, is ethically defensible when it involves participants in a mutual quest for excellence. In effect, competitors should view themselves as under a moral obligation to their opponents. Each competitor is obligated to try his or her best, so that opponents can develop their own skills and be genuinely tested. On this view, sports are absorbing to spectator and participant alike precisely because they involve both our minds and bodies so fully in meeting a challenge, a challenge worth meeting for its own sake.

While there are different levels of competitive intensity, even the weekend athlete playing in an informal and relaxed atmosphere tries to play well and fantasizes about making great plays. Who has not imagined himself or herself as a major league player instead of an outfielder on the last place team in the B level intramural league. What hacker on the golf course, after hitting a rare good shot, has not said (although not usually out loud) "Jack Nicklaus himself couldn't have hit it any better." Thus, even in relaxed informal play, the ethic of the mutual quest for excellence has application. What distinguishes the fun we have through sports from mere exercise is the presence of standards of excellence and the challenge provided by the play of others.

At the professional and semiprofessional levels, the personal goals of players and coaches may be primarily financial. The danger there becomes that sports will degenerate into simply what sells. At its worst, crass professionalism can transform a sport into "show biz," as seems to have happened to professional wrestling. While such a product may sell, at least for a time, the beauty, drama, and value of athletic competition are lost. At their best, professional sports retain the ethic of competition as the mutual quest for excellence.

Many athletes at the highest levels of amateur and professional competition seem to love the challenge sports provide. They seem to compete as much for the love of competition as for the external rewards it provides. Indeed, it is hard to see how anyone could rise to the top in a highly competitive sport, without the love of the game and the dedication to excellence providing enormous motivation for the hours and hours of practice, drills, and preparation that are required.

At that level of intensity, the danger is that the drive for excellence will lead athletes to use dangerous and arguably unethical means to achieve success. Losing becomes identified with failure and anything which promotes winning acquires the aura of success.

Accordingly, we need to ask about the *means* by which excellence might be achieved. In this chapter, we will explore the morality of one means of achieving success in athletics. Is the use of drugs, such as anabolic steroids, an ethically defensible method for achieving excellence in sport?

## THE USE OF PERFORMANCE ENHANCING DRUGS

The relatively wide use of such drugs as anabolic steroids dates back at least to the Olympics of the nineteen sixties, although broad public awareness of use of such drugs seems comparatively recent. Anabolic steroids are drugs, synthetic derivatives of the hormone testosterone, that stimulate muscle growth and tissue repair. Although not everyone would agree that the controlled use of steroids to enhance performance is dangerous, the American College of Sports Medicine as well as other medical groups warn against serious side effects. These are believed to include, at least at high levels of dosage, liver damage, artherosclerosis, hypertension, and a lowered sperm count in males. The regular use of steroids also is asserted to produce such personality changes as increased aggressiveness and hostility.[1]

Although the degree to which steroids are used by top amateur and professional athletes naturally is unclear, virtually all observers would agree that it is not rare. Users range from weight lifters, to linemen in professional football to track and field stars. The Summer 1983 Pan American Games were disrupted, for example, when several gold medal winners, including Americans, were disqualified for the use of such performance enhancing drugs as steroids. In addition, many other athletes withdrew from events rather than take tests which might have revealed drug use. What is particularly frightening is that world class athletes are reported to be taking steroids at many times the recommended dosage. Such athletes are unlikely to be influenced by claims that steroid use has little effect on performance, when such claims are based on studies where only low doses of the relevant drugs were administered.

Perhaps the use of steroids to enhance athletic performance is imprudent, if the risk of serious side effects is high (although dedicated athletes might reply that if the use of drugs helps them attain their highest goals, use is not imprudent after all). Leaving issues of prudence aside for the moment, however, we need to consider whether the use of steroids to enhance athletic performance is unethical and, if so, on what grounds.

### The Case Against Steroids

Why shouldn't athletes be allowed to use steroids and other drugs which enhance performance? One argument against such use is that steroids are harmful to users, particularly at the high levels of dosage which might be required to enhance performance in sport. Is this claim sufficient to support a prohibition on the use of steroids by athletes?

Let us accept the factual premise that the steroid use can be harmful, although at least some of the evidence, particularly of psychological effects, tends to be anecdotal. Indeed, even if there are risks involved in the use of performance-enhancing drugs, they may be less significant than the risks involved in playing such contact sports as football or boxing.[2]

However, even if we accept the claim that the use of steroids involves significant risk, it does not follow that the use of steroids may be prohibited. If the prohibition is *paternalistic,* designed to protect athletes from harming themselves, doesn't it violate their liberty? If athletes prefer the gains the use of steroids provide along with risk of possible side effects to the alternative of less risk but worse performance, what warrants any outside agency with interfering with their personal choice?

But while considerations of personal liberty appear to undermine the logical basis for condemnation of the use of steroids, we should not accept such a conclusion too quickly. Let us examine the preceding arguments more closely first.

### Informed Consent and the Use of Steroids

As we have seen, there are strong reasons for opposing paternalistic interference with the self-regarding actions of competent adults. However, it is far from clear that those reasons apply in full force to the use of steroids.

In particular, we need to consider whether the decision by highly competitive athletes to use steroids really is a free choice. Second, even if such a choice is free, we need to consider whether it really is self-regarding or whether it limits the freedom of others in improper ways.

Normally, it is unethical to coerce competent adults into taking drugs without their informed consent.[3] However, if the athlete has given informed consent to administration of a performance-enhancing drug, then the antipaternalistic arguments summarized above apply. Is it reasonable to think, however, that most of the athletes who take anabolic steroids have given informed consent to their use?

Consider the case of professional sports. The professional athlete's livelihood may depend on performing at the highest level. Athletes who are not among the very best in the world at their work may not be professional athletes very long. "Thus, the onus is on the athlete to continue playing and to consent to things that he or she would not otherwise consent to. . . . Coercion, however subtle, makes the athlete vulnerable. It also takes away the athlete's ability to act and choose freely with regard to informed consent."[4]

However, while this point does not lack all force, the use of the term "coercion" can be questioned. After all, no one is literally forced to become a professional athlete. If we want to use "coercion" so broadly, are we committed to saying that coaches coerce players into lifting weights or practicing hard? Do professors "coerce" students into doing homework? Isn't it more plausible to say that while there are pressures in sport to achieve maximum physical conditioning, these no more amount to coercion than do the pressures on law or medical students to study hard? After all, if one doesn't like the heat, one can always leave the kitchen.

We do need to be careful of loose use of the word "coercion." Is it really more plausible to think that most top athletes who use steroids are the victims of coercion or that they have made a decision about what risks are reasonable to take in light of potential gains? At the very least, we are not entitled to assume that professional athletes are unable to give informed consent unless we are willing to count similar pressures in other professions as forms of coercion as well. If we use "coercion" that broadly, it becomes unclear who, if anybody, is left free.

Of course, there may be borderline cases where pressures from teammates and owners to take a drug are unusually severe. Or perhaps an athlete reluctant to take drugs is actually threatened by someone in power. In such cases, either coercion may be present or, if not, the situation may still be unusual enough that we doubt that the decision is free enough to be a valid case of consent. There may be degrees of pressure which, once a certain point is approached, allow for reasonable concern about the ability of persons to consent. So while we cannot conclude that top athletes, even professional athletes, are incapable of giving informed consent in general, there may be grounds for concern in particular cases.[5]

It sometimes is argued that even if some sophisticated athletes do give informed consent, the fact of their drug use may force others, who would not otherwise do so, into taking steroids. Some athletes may feel that unless they take such drugs, they will be unable to compete. If they don't take steroids, they will be placing themselves at a disadvantage relative to those who do. Just as a student may study harder than she originally planned on a test because her classmates are studying extra hard, so the world class athlete may turn to drugs in order to keep up with opponents she believes are already users.[6] Athletes feel trapped into becoming drug users; if they don't use drugs they believe their performances will not be competitive.[7] Such externally imposed competitive pressures unjustifiably interfere with the athlete's pursuit of excellence and coerce top performers into using drugs.

However, while the existence of such competitive pressures cannot be denied, it is unclear that the imposition of these kinds of pressure on opponents is *improper* or *unethical* interference with their lives. As one writer argues, "The ingestion of steroids for competitive reasons cannot be distinguished from the other tortures, deprivations and risks to which athletes subject themselves to achieve success. No one is coerced into world class competition. . . . If they find the costs excessive, they may withdraw."[8]

However, while it is true that athletes are free to drop out of competition if they find that the costs outweigh the benefits, are all kinds of competitive pressures morally equivalent? Suppose one's co-workers chose to put in extra hours on the job. Their decision may increase the pressure on you to work overtime, if only to show your employer that you are as dedicated as your colleagues to your work. Such pressures do not seem coercive or illegitimate. But now suppose your fellow workers take dangerous stimulants to allow them to put even more hours into their work. Your employer then asks why you aren't working as hard as they are. You reply that you can only keep up the pace by taking the stimulant and endangering your health. Is the employer's reply, "Well, no one's forcing you to stay on the job, but if you stay you'd better put in as many hours as the others" really acceptable?

Although many of us may be intuitively inclined to say the cases differ, it is hard to say where the relevant difference lies. After all, the stress generated by extra work may damage health even if stimulants are not taken. Is it simply the extra risk generated by drug use that worries us? (If so, we can simply change the example so that each kind of pressure generates equivalent risk.) Or is there something about the use of drugs as opposed to plain old fashioned elbow grease that bothers us?

In sports at least, there may well be something illegitimate about achievements attained through the use of drugs. Before turning to that point, however, there is another factor which warrants consideration. If the use of performance-enhancing drugs becomes widespread at top levels of athletic competition, it is virtually sure to filter down to lower and ever lower age groups. Perhaps interference with the liberties of top athletes is warranted to protect others, particularly children and teenagers, who are not yet competent and responsible adults, from the competitive pressures to become users.

We can conclude, then, that although considerations of informed consent do not provide conclusive grounds for a prohibition of the use of performance-enhancing drugs, concern about the pressures users place on others is not entirely unwarranted either. The challenge, which we have not yet met, is to articulate a principle which specifies a morally relevant difference between the effects of steroid use on other competitors and, say, the effects of an equally risky conditioning program on other competitors. Until that challenge is met, while concern for others, particularly youngsters, provides a reason for favoring a prohibition of steroid use, it remains unclear whether that reason is sufficiently weighty to carry the day.

The case against use is strengthened, however, if we consider not only whether athletes *consent* to the use of steroids but also whether they are likely to be *informed* about possible adverse consequences. Although many sophisticated athletes may be aware of the risks they run, others surely are not. The younger and more unsophisticated the player, the less likely is the decision to take steroids to be reflective and informed.

Perhaps the most warranted conclusions to emerge from our discussion of informed consent are these. First, there are philosophical difficulties confronting the opponent of steroid use who argues from the absence of informed consent. Nevertheless, doubts about informed consent are not totally without force. While inconclusive in themselves, they may, when conjoined with other factors, constitute strong support for a prohibition of the use of performance-enhancing drugs in sport.

### Steroids and the Ethics of Competition

There is another ethical difficulty with the use of such performance-enhancing drugs as steroids. If competition in sport is supposed to be a test of the athletic abilities, both mental and physical, of *persons,* is the very nature of competition undermined if artificial aids to performance are introduced? Presumably, we would not accept a new track record made while the runner wore special mechanical shoes that added extra spring to his strides. Neither would we accept a record golf score made with the aid of an illegal "hot" ball that traveled further than the rules allow. The reason we refuse to accept such records, I suggest, is that they do not reflect the talents of the athletes but the quality of their equipment. Of course, we could allow every competitor to use the new equipment. However, this should not be permitted when technological advances in equipment would undermine the nature of the game itself. Surely shoes which mechanically add spring to a runner's strides or golf balls which are so "hot" that they make even the longest courses seem short fall under such a heading.

Why wouldn't the same argument apply to performance-enhancing drugs? Where such drugs lead to improved play, it is not the person who is responsible for the gain? Rather, it is the drug which makes the difference. How does this differ from the case where the souped-up golf ball, rather than improvement in the player, leads to a record-breaking score?

If this suggestion has force, it is because the goal of competition in sport is not simply to achieve excellence. Rather, it is to meet *as a person* the test presented by the abilities of an opponent or the qualities of an athletic obstacle, such as a ski slope or golf course. The good competitor does not see opponents as bodies, as things to be beaten down, but as persons whose acts constitute a mutually acceptable challenge and which call for appropriate response.

At this point, critics might object that steroids are not magic pills which guarantee success regardless of the qualities of the user. Athletes using steroids must practice as hard or harder than others to attain the full benefits of use. So in a contest among users, it is still personal qualities that would determine who wins and who loses.

Leaving aside the points made earlier about informed consent—particularly the fear that use by some would place unwarranted pressure on others to do the same—this reply still is not satisfactory. Thus, if a point of weight lifting, for example, is to test the limits of human strength and courage, how can it continue to fulfill such a function if what really is being tested is the limits of drug enhanced strength and courage? After all, we also could give each competitor a special machine that lifted the first fifty pounds mechanically. What would be the point?

A persistent critic might still object, however. According to such a person, the introduction of steroids does not differ from other technological advances that have been accepted in sport. Changes have been allowed in the equipment of pole vaulters, tennis players, and golfers, all of which have led to improved performance. How does the use of steroids differ?

Leaving aside once again our earlier fears about informed consent, a reply is still possible. New equipment must be used *by the athlete*. Since such equipment is theoretically available to all, it is the qualities of the individual athletes and teams that make the difference in competition. What drugs do, however, is change the qualities of the athletes themselves. What is being tested is not the limits of human performance, but of drug-enhanced performance.

Of course, that may be what we want to test for. We could make performance-enhancing drugs available to all athletes just as new lightweight clubs are available to all golfers. But what do we gain? What we lose is clear. Successful performance in sport would no longer reflect skill, motivation, courage, and other virtues, but would be determined in part by drugs. After all, the golfer still must hit the shot even with improved clubs, but what would be the point of golf if we could give all golfers a drug that would make them swing correctly every time, regardless of the psychological pressures and physical difficulties facing them. If we want to go that far, why not genetically engineer weight lifters, runners, and high jumpers, or even better, substitute competition among robot athletes for competition among persons?

If the goal of achieving excellence in performance becomes overriding, so that the activity of persons facing challenges in sport becomes secondary, we may be led to the absurd conclusion that since humans cannot achieve the theoretical limits of top performance, lets get them out of sport altogether. If we are willing to change the very nature of athletes through steroids, why not replace human athletes altogether with mechanically or biologically engineered super-athletes who can do the job even better?

Perhaps one could respond that even normal conditioning programs "change the nature of the athlete" and so do not differ in the relevant respect from steroid use. But while further discussion undoubtedly is needed to make a more conclusive case, perhaps enough has been said to put the burden of proof on advocates of the use of steroids. After all, the effects of conditioning depend on the dedication and innate qualities of the athlete while drugs provide an unearned bonus which is irrelevant to the qualities and skills that should be valued in sport.

There seem to be two good reasons, then, for supporting the prohibition of the use of performance-enhancing drugs from organized competition in sport. First, there sometimes is reason to believe that some athletes are not in the position to give informed consent to drug use. Second, the ethics of good competition require us to meet the challenges set by opponents *as persons*. Arguably, performance-enhancing drugs violate this principle of good sport.

### What is a Drug?

Even if the above conclusions are sound, many fundamental questions remain. For example, we may agree that the use of performance-enhancing drugs should be prohibited. But what is to count as such a drug?

Should athletes be prohibited from taking heavy doses of vitamins? What about special diets, such as the carbohydrate binge indulged in by many long distance runners? A particularly bizarre practice involves runners storing their own blood in a frozen state and then returning the red blood cells to the body. The elevated red cell content theoretically enables the body to send more oxygen to the muscles, resulting in enhanced performance. Should such "blood doping" be forbidden, perhaps because of reasons similar to those developed above? On the other hand, how can one's own blood be considered a drug?

Unfortunately, there do not seem to be any simple principles which distinguish improper performance-enhancing drugs from legitimate training diets or the moderate use of vitamins. Thus, it is no help to say that athletes should be permitted to take only what is "natural," since steroids contain the natural hormone testosterone, while many legitimate medications are synthetic or at least not present in the normal diet. The concept of "natural" is too vague and open-ended to bear the weight the proposed distinction places upon it. Clearly, there are great theoretical and practical problems involved in any attempt to draw a line between what is and what is not permissible. The best approach might be to take things on a case-by-case (or substance-by-substance) approach, letting general principles emerge inductively from our intuitive responses to specific problems. Our discussion suggests that a fundamental requirement is to distinguish, between training techniques, diet and medication that maximize the health of the athletes so that they can fulfil their maximum potential and drugs which alter performance in ways that do not reflect the behavior of the athlete *qua* person. The intuitive idea here is that performance should reflect the athlete's skills, choices and motivation. In any case, rather than begin with a formal definition of "performance enhancing drug," we first need to decide an ethical issue; namely, what kinds of factors *ought* or *ought not* to be allowed to affect athletic performance.


## ENFORCEMENT

If rules banning the use of performance-enhancing drugs are to be effective, they must be enforced. Enforcement, however, involves a host of ethical issues. Presumably, drug use will be detected by medical procedures involving blood tests. But can athletes be forced to take such tests? What about informed *consent?* What about civil libertarian concerns about self-incrimination, particularly in cases where tests are not fully reliable and are capable of detecting use of such illegal substances as cocaine?

### The Ethics of Testing

Athletic organizations such as the International Olympic Committee have no moral authority to force persons to undergo medical procedures. To impose such a procedure on a competent adult against his or her will is tantamount to committing battery upon the affected individual. On the other hand, athletic organizations are free to set their own eligibility conditions for competition. While no one can be tested without consent, those who do not consent need not be permitted to compete either.

Of course, such organizations should not set up totally arbitrary eligibility requirements. They have no right to require that athletes provide intimate details of their sex lives, for example. The requirements must be *relevant* to the purposes of athletic competition. If the arguments advanced in previous sections are sound, testing for use of performance-enhancing drugs is relevant to the function of such organizations as the Olympic

Committee. After all, their role is to insure that the competitions they organize are fair.

However, there are grounds for doubting that tests will actually promote fair competition or protect the health of athletes. Clever athletes, aided by scientists who may be employed by governments in pursuit of Olympic victories, may devise more and more sophisticated ways to "beat" the tests. Users may be driven underground, at more and more risk to their health. At least some athletes believe that a nonpunitive policy, which attempts to minimize drug use through education and dissemination of information, may be more effective in the long run than a blanket prohibition based on the fear of getting caught.[9]

But while long-range consequences always are difficult to estimate with confidence, considerations of fairness in competition, along with the doubts expressed earlier about informed consent, seem to count in favor of testing. However, if testing is employed, athletes from all countries should be required to take part, not just for the Olympics, but in major competitions at national levels as well. Thus, athletes in the United States should be faced with a common drug policy. Testing should not be restricted to the Olympics, but should apply to top intercollegiate and other major amateur competitions. Otherwise, we risk getting into the position, for example, of finding that what is considered fair by the NCAA is considered unfair by the Olympic Committee. Such multiple standards can only confuse athletes and call into question the integrity of competition at different levels of sport.

Testing for drugs does raise important issues of civil liberties. What if the tests are not fully reliable? Can an innocent person be mistakenly disqualified on the basis of a questionable test result? Are there fair procedures for appeal?

These issues are particularly acute if we widen the net to include tests for use of illegal "recreational" drugs, such as cocaine, or alcohol abuse. Indeed, if the NFL can require its players to take tests which reveal cocaine use, why can't other employers do the same? True, fans of professional sports pay to see the best possible performance, while regular use of such drugs as cocaine may adversely affect athletic efficiency. But the ordinary car owner also pays the repair facility for efficient performance, which also may be adversely affected if workers are drug users. Indeed, loss of worker efficiency caused by drug use already is a major national problem.[10] If we permit widespread testing in sport, are we setting a precedent for its use throughout society? What protection is needed against unreliable tests, misinterpretation of data, and violation of privacy? On the other hand, don't employers and consumers alike have a justified claim to get what they paid for from employees? What if the safety or productivity of some employees depends on the efficiency of others, a factor which may be even more important in high risk construction work or medicine than in football?

While we cannot explore these broader social questions here, there does seem to be a case based on public safety and fairness to fellow workers for the use of tests in some areas of employment. That case seems especially strong at the top levels of amateur and professional sports, particularly where the use of performance-enhancing drugs is at issue. After all, no one is forced to participate in sport at high levels of competition, and the rewards for success can be very great. Athletes have a right to expect fair competition, which would preclude some competitors gaining an advantage over others by the secret use of such drugs as steroids. Such drugs are not used by athletes in the private pursuit of pleasure. Rather, they are used to gain a competitive advantage in sport. If we conclude, as it has been argued above, that there are good reasons for disallowing such an advantage, authorities are entitled to enforce such a prohibition. Indeed as we have seen, it can be doubted whether informed consent can be given under such circumstances. Thus, not only can testing be defended as a means of protecting the fairness of competition, it also can be justified as a safeguard of the liberty of athletes rather than than an infringement upon their freedom.

While the nature of enlightened drug policy in sports needs far more consideration than we have given it here, the following general principles have been supported by our discussion.

1.  The use of performance-enhancing drugs such as steroids by some competitors violates canons of fair competition, may fail to respect the principle of informed consent, and places undue pressure on other athletes to become users themselves.

2.  Although testing for drug use does raise important questions for civil liberties, some testing at the highest levels of competitive sport may be permissible to insure fair competition and preserve the integrity of athletic contests.

While complexities remain, the use of performance-enhancing drugs is antithetical to the ethics of good competition in sports. In addition, there is a risk that their use will involve disrespect for athletes as persons who must not be treated with drugs in the absence of informed consent. Thus, we are entitled to conclude that the use of drugs by competitors should be prohibited and the prohibition enforced, by testing if necessary.[11]

## NOTES

[1]See Terry Todd, "The Steroid Predicament," *Sports Illustrated*, August 1, 1983, pp. 71-72, for a sensitive interview with an athlete and his wife on what they believe to be the effects of steroid use on their marriage.

[2]This point is made by Norman Fost in "Let 'Em Take Steroids," *The New York Times*, Sept. 9, 1983, p A19. ©1983 by The New York Times Company. Reprinted by permission.

[3]For a discussion and summary of the literature of informed consent and the role it plays in medical ethics, see Terrance C. McConnell, *Moral Issues in Health Care: An Introduction to Medical Ethics* (Monterey, Calif.: Wadsworth Health Sciences Division, 1982), Chap. 3.

[4]Carolyn E. Thomas, *Sport in a Philosophic Context,* (Philadelphia: Lea & Febiger, 1983), p. 198.

[5]The well-publicized Bill Walton case is such an instance. Walton, a star basketball player on the Portland Trail Blazers was given pain killers to enable him to participate in the NBA playoffs. Walton severely injured his foot in competition, perhaps because the drugs masked painful warning signs that he was not physically ready to participate. The case is discussed by David Halberstam in *The Breaks of the Game* (New York: Random House, 1981).

[6]Fred Dwyer, "The Real Problem: Using Drugs to Win," *The New York Times,* July 4, 1982, p. 2S.

[7]Todd, "The Steroid Predicament," p. 76.

[8]Fost, "Let 'Em Take Steroids."

[9]For such an argument, see Harold Connolly, "Drug Testing Cannot Insure Fair Play," *The New York Times,* Sept. 4, 1983, p. 2S.

[10]For a general discussion of the effects of drugs in the workplace, see "Taking Drugs on the Job," *Newsweek,* August 22, 1983, pp. 52-60.

[11]For a discussion which diverges from the conclusions of this chapter, see W. M. Brown, "Ethics, Drugs and Sports," *Journal of the Philosophy of Sport,* Vol 7, 1980, pp. 15-23.

# CHAPTER FIVE
# EQUALITY
# AND EXCELLENCE
# IN SPORTS

In Chapters Two, Three, and Four an attempt has been made to develop, defend, and apply an ethic of competition in sports and athletics. In the next two chapters, our concern will shift from examination of ethical principles that should regulate good competition in sport to an examination of the rights and entitlements of participants. Are there fundamental rights to share in the benefits of participation in sport? Does everyone have a right to play? Does the greater ability of some entitle them to more rewards than others? Does implementation of sex equality in sport require the elimination of sexual distinctions or does it require separate athletic competitions for men and women? In addressing these and related questions, issues involving the scope and nature of rights, the significance of equality, and the meaning of equity and social justice will face us. In addressing them, we will consider not only basic questions about fairness and equality in sport, but broader questions about the just and equitable society as well.

Throughout our discussion, it has been argued that competition in sports is ethically defensible when it involves a mutual quest for excellence among competitors. However, while we considered briefly in Chapter Two whether the inequality created by the division of winners and losers was morally objectionable, broader questions about equality remain to be considered. In particular, we have not considered the question of equal access to athletic participation and facilities. Do people have *rights* to participate in sport and share in the goods that participation promotes? Are communities obligated to provide facilities, such as swimming pools, so that everyone has a chance to participate. Or are individuals only entitled to what they can purchase on the open market? We also need to consider whether emphasis on competition discourages participation by placing too much premium on achievement and too little on having fun. Finally, we have not considered whether the special rewards that go to the athletically talented are justified. Does emphasis on competition as the mutual quest for excellence undermine legitimate concern for greater equality in sports?

Each of our questions involves the concept of *equality*. The first concerns whether individuals have equal rights to the benefits of sports. The second concerns whether emphasis on competition promotes unequal participation, and suggests that more equal participation should be an important goal of social policy with respect to sport. Finally, the third question concerns what degree of significance should be attached to inequalities of talent and ability. This chapter, then, is an investigation of the ethics of equality in sports policy.

As we have seen in Chapter Two, although the concept of equality has to do with sameness, there can be different conceptions of the role equality should play in social policy. "Equality," for example, can refer at least to nondiscrimination on sexual or racial grounds, to providing the same background opportunities for all, to showing the same respect and concern for everyone, or to providing the identical distribution of goods and services to each person.

In much recent discussion, equality is identified with equity, justice, and the good society. Often when a term is used that broadly, it comes to mean different things to different people. But from the fact that we all may favor equality, it doesn't follow that we favor the same policies, for, as we have seen, different conceptions of equality compete for our allegiance. Indeed, some cases of equal treatment clearly are unjust. An instructor who gives a poor student and an excellent student the same grade may be treating them equally in one sense, but is not treating them equitably. Equality is not necessarily identical with equity, fairness, or social justice.

In this chapter, then, we will not only explore the implications of concern for equality in sport, and the role it plays in the ideal of competition as the mutual quest for excellence. We will investigate the scope and limits of equality in social policy as well.

In particular, three specific questions concerning equality in sport will be pursued in this chapter.

1.  Do individuals have rights to benefits of participation in sport?
2.  Should more equal participation in sport be a goal of sports policy in America?
3.  Is it unjust to assign unequal rewards on the basis of unequal performance in sports and athletics?

## SPORTS AND SOCIAL JUSTICE

In his provocative and readable book, *Sports In America,* the noted author James Michener argues that our society lavishes far too much attention on the star athlete at the expense of the ordinary person. According to Michener,

> We place an undue emphasis on gifted athletes fifteen to twenty-two, a preposterous emphasis on a few professionals aged twenty-three to thirty-five, and never enough on the mass of our population aged twenty-three to seventy-five.[1]

Michener proposes instead that "The goals of American sports must be to provide every man or woman an equitable opportunity to develop his or her skills to the maximum capacity."[2]

There is much to be said for the charge of overemphasis on the skills of a talented elite. Top professional sports stars receive far more in salary than nurses, teachers, scientific researchers, and even the President of the United States. Large universities devote far more funds to their intercollegiate athletic programs than to providing a sound program of physical education for the majority of their students. At the high school or elementary school level, far more attention may be paid to developing the skills of top players than to insuring that the greater number of students learn to enjoy sports and to achieve good physical conditioning. Even in organized children's sports, the best young players often receive the most playing time at the more demanding positions while many less talented youngsters spend the better part of the season watching from the bench.

The end result seems to be that in spite of a much publicized fitness "boom," most Americans do not get sufficient exercise for good health. Moreover, rates of participation in some form of exercise or athletics may well vary along socioeconomic lines. As observers have noted, the current emphasis on jogging and exercise may be largely a middle- and upper-class phenomenon.[3]

The costs of such lack of fitness are both personal and social. Roughly one out of five American males has a heart attack by age 60, a much, much higher rate than for most of the world. Although the statistics are better for women, many experts think lack of exercise can contribute to heart attacks in females as well as males. While experts disagree about just what causes many ailments, there does seem to be agreement that improper diet and lack of proper exercise can contribute to the inception and severity of many illnesses.

On the other hand, participation in sports can contribute to the enjoyment of life in a variety of ways other than through direct effects upon health. For example, studies of female athletes suggest that such women have a more positive self-image and a greater sense of well-being than nonathletes.[4] Most important there is the pleasure of athletic activity itself, which too many of us only rarely experience in the daily course of our lives.

In the passage quoted earlier, James Michener suggests that America should have a *policy* towards sports. In particular, that policy should be one of encouraging mass participation in sports and athletics. The direction should be away from overemphasizing rewards for a talented few and on involving the greater number in enjoyable and healthy athletic activity. Let us examine some of the implications of this claim.

What Michener leaves unclear is whether he thinks our sports practices simply are *less good* than they ought to be, perhaps because they produce less satisfaction for the bulk of the population than is feasible, or whether they are *unjust* in that they violate individual rights or entitlements. It is important to distinguish questions of individual rights and social justice, on one hand, from issues involving desirable social policy, on the other. An injustice involves violation of a central area of personal integrity or individual right which is not justifiable even if it benefits the greater number. Rather, justice, and the individual rights it protects, *limits* the methods we may use in pursuing benefits. Thus, it would be unjust to silence unpopular speakers or prevent people we disagree with from voting even if such practices would efficiently promote certain goals, such as election of the best candidates. As one writer has put it, rights function as political trumps which individuals can play to protect their fundamental concerns against encroachment, even when such encroachment is favored by the majority.[5]

Is Michener, in the passage quoted earlier, making a claim about social justice and individual rights, or is he making a claim about desirable social policy? Is he arguing that greater participation and more equality in sports is desirable because it would produce many benefits, such as a healthier and happier work force? Or is he implying that individuals have rights in relations to sports and that a society which does not honor such rights is in some way unjust? Michener himself is not explicit on these points but the difference is crucial. Although it is undesirable for a society to be inefficient, it is morally prohibited, except perhaps in extreme emergencies, for it to violate the rights of individuals. Is sports policy in America seriously unjust?

## EQUALITY AND FREEDOM IN SPORTS

### Basic and Scarce Benefits

What benefits arise from sports? Do all individuals have equal rights to such benefits? If not, how should the benefits be distributed?

It is useful to begin with a distinction suggested by the late Jane English, formerly professor of philosophy at the University of North Carolina, in her article "Sex Equality in Sports." English suggests that we distinguish *basic benefits* of participation in sports from *scarce benefits.* Basic benefits are available to all participants, and their possession by some does not preclude their possession by others. Among such basic benefits are

> health, the self-respect to be gained from doing one's best, the cooperation to be learned from working with teammates and the incentive to be gained from having opponents, the "character" of learning to be a good loser and a good winner, the chance to improve one's skills and learn to accept criticism—and just plain fun.[6]

Scarce benefits, on the other hand, cannot be equally available to all. Their possession by some precludes possession, or at least equal possession, by others. The principal scarce goods of sports are fame and fortune: if everyone is equally famous or has equal wealth, then no one is famous and no one has a fortune. Fame and fortune, by their very nature, are comparative.[7]

When Michener and other writers complain that sports in America revolves too greatly around the achievements of an athletic elite, they can be read as claiming that the basic benefits of sports should be more widely distributed. In examining this claim, let us first consider whether individuals have rights to basic benefits. If so, a society that does not provide such benefits to its citizens when it is able to do so is unjust.

### Rights and Basic Benefits

Do all individuals have equal rights to the basic benefits of participation in sport, as Jane English suggested?[8] Such a view seems at least initially plausible. While unequal merit or unequal ability might entitle better athletes to special rewards, it does not seem to entitle them to an extra share of basic benefits. Top players do not deserve more fun or better health than others simply because of their superior skills or performance in athletics.

However, before agreeing too quickly that all individuals have equal rights to the basic benefits, we need to consider just what having a right might entail. Although philosophers disagree about just how rights are to be analyzed, there is wide agreement that rights impose obligations. For example, if I have a right to speak freely on a college campus, others on that campus are obligated to refrain from interfering with my speech. Similarly, if I have a right to medical care, some person(s) must be under an obligation to provide me with appropriate medical attention.[9] Thus, to understand the force of a rights claim, it is crucial to understand what obligations it imposes and upon whom the obligations are imposed. While rights may constitute a benefit to the bearers, they may impose significant burdens on others as well.

On one hand, rights may be understood *negatively.* On this view, they require only that people be left alone to pursue the basic benefits for themselves if they so choose. Negative rights obligate others only to refrain from interfering with our pursuit of the basic goods. Positive obligations, such as the obligation to pay taxes for support of recreational facilities, are not imposed.

If we understand the alleged right to the basic benefits of sport in this way, it is relatively uncontroversial. On this interpretation, the right to the basic benefits is a special instance of our fundamental right to liberty. That right obligates others only to refrain from interfering with our freedom, which is limited in turn only by the basic rights of others. But while such a right is relatively uncontroversial, it also is quite undemanding. It obligates us only to leave others alone. As such, it provides little basis for criticism of sports in America, since it demands so little of us. The alleged negative right to the basic benefits of sports is simply liberty to pursue them. It does not require that anyone actually attain the benefits.

However, the claim that individuals have a right to the basic benefits can be understood in a different and more controversial way. On this second interpretation, it may impose *positive* obligations on others to actually provide the basic benefits to rights bearers. If we construe the right to basic benefits as a positive right, we cannot say we are honoring it just by leaving others alone. Rather, we must do something specific to insure their possession of the basic benefits. This is an important point for, as we will see, it is all too easy to use the rhetoric of positive rights while forgetting that such rights can impose onerous costs on others. This point is one foundation of the political position known as Libertarianism.

### Rights and Liberties

What sort of costs would implementation of the positive right to basic benefits impose on others? Consider, for example, one of the basic benefits cited by Jane English; namely, the incentive to be gained from having opponents. Clearly, if one has a positive right to such a good, then someone must be obligated to serve as an opponent. But surely opponents are persons in their own right who should be left free to decide whom they wish to play against or whether they wish to play at all. A similar point applies to alleged rights to participate with coaches and teammates. They too are persons who cannot be "drafted" simply to please others. Here we need to keep in mind Robert Nozick's reminder that "The major objection to speaking of everyone's having a right *to* various things . . . is that these 'rights' require a substructure of things and materials and actions; and *other* people may have rights and entitlements over these."[10]

Carried to what many would regard as an unjustifiable extreme, this criticism of positive rights evolves into a position known as *Libertarianism*. According to Libertarianism, interference with the liberty of others is morally prohibited, except when necessary to preserve the right to liberty itself. Accordingly, while Libertarians will accept the police functions of the state, which are held to be necessary for the protection of negative liberty, Libertarians reject the welfare state. In their view, such a state is an example of Orwell's Big Brother. It constantly interferes with our liberty to control our property by using the tax system to force us to benefit others.

Robert Nozick has used his widely discussed Wilt Chamberlain example to illustrate the Libertarian complaint against redistribution for purposes of implementing a favored pattern of benefits throughout society. According to this example, we are to suppose that goods have already been redistributed throughout society according to our own ideal pattern of justice, whatever it turns out to be, for example, equality. Suppose further that a talented athlete, such as former basketball great Wilt Chamberlain, sets up a series of professional games. According to contract, Wilt is to get $.25 out of every $1.00 paid for admissions. It turns out that a million people pay $1.00 each to see Wilt play. As a result, Wilt ends up $250,000 richer and each spectator ends up $1.00 poorer. The initial pattern of equality is shattered.

What is the point of this example? According to Nozick,

> The general point illustrated by the . . . example . . . is that no . . . distributional patterned principle of justice can be continuously realized without continuous interference with people's lives. . . . To maintain a pattern one must either continually interfere to stop people from transferring resources as they wish to, or continually (or periodically) interfere to take from some persons resources that others . . . wish to transfer to them.[11]

Applied to sports, the Chamberlain example can be cited in support of the claim that realization of positive rights to the basic benefits interferes unduly with the liberty of others.

### Objections to Libertarianism

Is Libertarianism an acceptable political philosophy? While this question is too large to deal with adequately here, two central criticisms of Libertarianism are particularly relevant to our inquiry. First, neither the Chamberlain example nor Nozick's warning about the limitations of positive rights are sufficient to justify Libertarianism. Second, there are good reasons for believing that the Libertarian rejection of positive rights is highly arbitrary given the values of the Libertarians themselves.

At most, the Chamberlain example shows that maintaining a fixed distributional *pattern* requires extensive interference with individual liberty.[12] However, it is possible to reject Libertarianism and endorse some positive rights without being committed to a fixed distributional pattern. For example, one might hold that everyone has a positive right to a minimally decent standard of living but maintain that so long as no one falls below such a welfare floor or safety net, other goods may be distributed according to individual choice as expressed within a free market. The tax system could be used to redistribute some share of wealth to keep the safety net in place but not to enforce a patterned distribution of wealth across society.

Similarly, Nozick is quite right to warn us to be careful that positive rights claims do not cover goods to which others already have a right. Thus, we have seen that no athlete can have a right to an opponent, for the potential opponents have rights to determine for themselves whether or not they want to compete. But it does not follow from this that *any* taxation for purposes of social welfare is unjust. Even if we have no right to a tennis opponent, we may have a right to a basic education or a decent diet. While the Libertarian is correct to point out that some claimed positive rights ought to be rejected because they impose too great a burden on others, it remains to be seen whether all positive rights can be rejected on similar grounds.

Indeed, upon reflection, we may reject the Libertarian's claim that the only fundamental moral rights are negative ones. This is because any Libertarian who is not an anarchist concedes that the state's function is to protect the liberty of its citizens. But in order to do this, the state must raise revenues to support a police force and a military establishment, as well as a judicial system. So even the Libertarian acknowledges that the good citizen must do more than simply let others alone. In addition, the good citizen has a positive obligation to provide support for institutions that protect negative rights. Isn't it arbitrary, then, for the Libertarian to claim that positive rights violate liberty while accepting some positive rights (for example, to police protection), nevertheless?[13]

A similar point can be made about property rights. Even the Libertarian is likely to admit that your right to property does not entail that you may light a fire in your yard which sends smoke into his living room or that you may drive your car through a residential area at any speed you wish. A court system clearly is needed to adjudicate the limits of property rights. But then citizens will have positive obligations to contribute to the maintenance of the judicial system.

While this is hardly sufficient to refute the entire Libertarian approach, it does show that the Libertarian faces significant objections. However, even if such objections turn out to be decisive, we cannot conclude that every individual has positive rights to the basic benefits of sport. Such rights may be too intrusive of the liberty of others. It remains to be seen whether any right to the basic benefits of sport can be shown to be so fundamental as to warrant inclusion within the safety net which every just society should provide for its citizens. So even if Libertarianism is not fully acceptable as a political philosophy, objections that specific rights to the basic benefits of sport intrude too greatly on the individual may have considerable force.

### Rights and Possibilities

There is a second difficulty with the idea of rights to the basic benefits of sports. Some basic benefits, such as good health or fun, are not fully or even largely subject to social control. This has important implications. We cannot have an obligation to provide health for others if it is beyond our powers to provide it. Similarly, how much fun one has may depend as much on one's own personality as on what others do. Since we cannot be obligated to provide what is beyond our control, positive rights claims *to* many of the basic benefits may be dismissed as logically absurd.

### Rights and Opportunities

In view of these objections, should we give up the claim that there are rights to the basic benefits of sports? Not necessarily. Perhaps we should follow the wording suggested by Michener and speak of *opportunity* to acquire the basic benefits rather than a right to the benefits themselves. The right to equal opportunity, as understood here, is more than a mere negative liberty. One can be at liberty to fly from Boston to San Francisco if no one will interfere, but have no real opportunity to go if there are no connecting flights. A right to opportunity may impose positive obligations on others, but normally these will be far less demanding than those imposed by rights to the basic benefits. After all, they are rights to a chance to acquire benefits, not to the benefits themselves.

What might a right to equal opportunity to acquire the basic benefits actually entail? While its exact content is controversial, it might at a minimum require schools to introduce children and young adults to the value of regular exercise, to promote fitness, and to teach "carry-over" sports, such as tennis, golf, and swimming, which can be pursued throughout a lifetime. The emphasis in such physical education programs would not be on producing future stars but on giving every child a genuine opportunity to strive for fitness and to participate in sports. Unfortunately, many school districts actually have cut back on physical education. Some of the remaining physical education programs, perhaps in an effort to be attractive to the physically unfit, have tended to emphasize recreation rather than fitness. For example, Proviso East High School in Maywood, Illinois, attracted national attention when it was learned its curriculum allowed students to play pinochle in P.E. class.[14]

A right to equal opportunity might also require communities to provide such facilities as parks, jogging paths and ball fields. Such a right also might entail provision of such public facilities as swimming pools, tennis courts, and golf courses, to say nothing of a paid recreational staff who supply instruction and supervision in a variety of activities.

However, there are grounds for not extending opportunity rights quite so far. The more extensive such rights are, the greater burden they impose on others. Even if we grant the existence of positive rights, it is doubtful that even a relatively affluent society is *unjust* if it fails to provide public golf courses, swimming pools, and professional recreational personnel. People who want such facilities often will be able to provide them for themselves. People who have no interest in sport will object that they should not be required to subsidize the play of those who do.

However, since human existence is social and not atomistically individualistic, we do not think it unjust to tax citizens who never use a museum or library in order to support such facilities. Moreover, opportunities for recreation and sport can be regarded as significant components of the good life. If one point of living in communities is to collectively provide elements of the good life which we can not always provide for ourselves, why can't the same case be made for provision of public athletic facilities as for cultural ones? After all, such facilities promote health, a stronger self-image, and expression of our status as persons through athletic competition.

Perhaps relatively affluent societies do owe it to their citizens to provide minimal opportunities, in terms of facilities and instruction, for healthy exercise. More extensive facilities may, but need not, be provided by each local community as it wishes. Those who strongly object to forced support of what they regard as amenities then have the choice to move to communities that don't provide them.

The Libertarian, then, is right to warn us against inflating the realm of rights. It is all too easy to slide from claims about what we want, or what would be good for us to have, to claims about what we are entitled to as a matter of right. The trouble with such inflated rights claims is that they impose too great a burden on others. On the other hand, Libertarianism as a comprehensive political philosophy faces severe criticism. It is doubtful if all positive rights claims can be rejected on Libertarian grounds.

If there are positive rights to a safety net, a right to *adequate* opportunities to participate in athletics needs to be included within it. The exercise such opportunities provide may be a prerequisite of good health for many people. Perhaps more important, the opportunities for play provided by sports are a significant element of a decent human life. Not only do sports provide a distinctive framework through which we can pursue excellence, they also provide a special medium through which we can express our nature as persons. On the other hand, provision of *extensive* opportunities and facilities, while desirable, should be left wherever possible to the choice of individuals or local communities. Accordingly, while the Libertarian's *a priori* rejection of all positive rights is questionable, we need not go to the other extreme by confusing what the ideal community might provide with the more modest requirements of social justice in sport.

## EQUALITY VS. EXCELLENCE IN SPORTS

Our discussion so far suggests that every individual has a moral right to some opportunities to exercise and participate in athletics. Such a right is derivable from each individual's claim to a minimally decent human existence, which includes opportunities to develop healthy living habits and to express basic human capacities and talents. While it is debatable how extensive such opportunities must be, affluent societies surely have greater responsibilities in this area than do less developed ones.

The opportunities in question involve chances to acquire the *basic* benefits of sports. However, we have seen that in addition to the basic benefits, such as fun and better health, there also are *scarce* benefits, such as fame and fortune. In our society, at virtually any level of competition, these scarce benefits go disproportionately to the talented and highly motivated athletes, not to the ordinary participant.

To many, such an unequal distribution seems self-evidently fair and just. After all, who should get the greatest rewards but the best and hardest-working individuals among us? But while such a view probably commands wide support, it is hardly free from significant criticism.

In particular, in the discussion that follows, two different kinds of criticism need to be kept in mind. The first, suggested in the passage quoted earlier from Michener, appeals to the allegedly bad *consequences* of adulation of an athletic elite. These include discouragement of the less talented, a resulting drop in participation, a less healthy population, a lower level of satisfaction throughout society than might otherwise be achieved, and reinforcement of inegalitarian status distinctions between high and low achievers. On this latter view, inequality in athletics serves only to support and reinforce inequality throughout the rest of society.

The second kind of criticism maintains that rewarding an athletically talented elite is not merely undesirable but also is *unjust*. For example, some writers have argued that it is unjust to reward individuals for natural gifts and talents with which they were born and for which they deserve no credit.

It will be useful to begin our discussion with consideration of organized sports for children. The critique of athletic elitism has considerable force in such a context. Whether such a critique has similar force when applied to highly competitive amateur and professional sports remains to be seen. Perhaps different standards of evaluation are appropriate to different levels of competition. If so, equality of participation may not be equally important in all kinds of athletic contests.

### Should John and Jane Warm the Bench?

According to many critics of organized sports for children, such as Little League baseball and Pop Warner football, too much emphasis is placed on a highly talented athletic elite and not enough on equal participation. Critics maintain that an overemphasis by parents and coaches on winning puts far too much pressure on young children. Since adults want to win, they assign highly skilled youngsters to the more demanding positions and give them the most instruction. Younger or less skilled players spend a disproportionate part of the season watching from the bench. When they do play, they seldom are given a chance to occupy key roles or positions.

As a result, it is charged that talented and untalented youngsters alike suffer harm, or at best derive only minimal benefits from participation. Less mature youngsters do not receive an adequate opportunity to develop their own skills, which might well come to surpass those of the early bloomers if only given a chance to develop. Even worse, such bench warmers might become so discouraged or humiliated that they lose all interest in sports, or develop a fear of participation, and never experience the basic benefits which participation in sports might provide. On the other hand, the more talented children can be placed under pressure too great for them to handle. Sports can cease to be fun and turn into work, carried out mainly to please adults. Young players may "freeze up," trying only to avoid making mistakes in front of parents or friends, rather than enjoying the competition or trying to improve skills. No wonder, then, that a number of top professional athletes have warned against overemphasis on competition and winning in organized children's sports.

This critique has considerable merit. The overbearing Little League parent and the coach who makes major league demands of children have become national stereotypes. However, national organizations as well as concerned parents and local groups have become more aware of dangers involved in excessive competition for youngsters, although many observers would say pressure is still far too intense.

Rather than debate how much competition is enough, a question about which reasonable people can be expected to disagree, it will be more useful to clarify the different values at stake in children's sports so that coaches, parents and children can make more informed decisions on their own.

We have already mentioned some of the dangers of overemphasis on winning and competition in children's sports. However, some of those who fear excessive competitiveness have a tendency to go to the opposite extreme and advocate complete equality of participation, regardless of its effects on good competition. Because they fear the effects of overemphasis on a young athletic elite, they are tempted to disregard obvious differences in ability and achievement. We should consider such a view, for we gain more appreciation of the values of competition and achievement if we examine what sports might be like in their absence. Let us, then, for purposes of analysis, consider an admittedly extreme version of the antielitist view; namely, the suggestion that every child be treated identically in organized children's sports.

While such a suggestion may seem superficially attractive, since it appears to give every child an equal chance to attain the basic benefits, it has clear and obvious weaknesses. For example, in baseball, not every child is physically capable of playing all the positions. It would be dangerous to assign a child who has difficulty catching to the position of first baseman or catcher. If a child with no control was made pitcher, every batter would walk while fielders could avoid boredom only by chasing butterflies.

There are more subtle difficulties as well with the suggestion we are considering. We need to consider the interests of the athletically skilled child as well as those of the beginner or less talented player. Just as academically gifted children may need special challenges in the classroom if their capacities are to develop to the maximum, athletically gifted children also may need special challenges in sports. In both academics and athletics, it would seem both unfair and inappropriate to treat gifted individuals as if their special abilities did not exist or were of no significance.

Moreover, it is important to remember that sports are more than mere exercise. In particular, standards of skillful performance have special weight in sports that they do not have in exercise. An essential part of learning to enjoy and appreciate sports is to learn to appreciate acts of skill by players. To the extent that identical treatment requires us to treat skill and excellence as if it did not exist, it requires us to ignore the very qualities instruction should help us develop. On the contrary, there is good reason for acknowledging outstanding performances, not only because we appreciate excellence, but also to help teach children and spectators to recognize and appreciate the exhibition of skill in sports. If this point is sound, one of the goals of sports for children should be not only to teach skills and encourage participation, but to develop the kind of appreciation of excellence which will provide enjoyment of sports throughout a lifetime.

Equal respect for all children who participate in organized sports does require that each youngster be given an equal opportunity to enjoy the basic benefits of participation. But *equal* opportunities need not be strictly *identical* ones. Thus, different levels of competition can be provided for those at different ability levels. Coaches can instruct each child, individualizing instruction to the child's skills. Many leagues now have rules requiring that each child on a team participate in games to a significant extent.

Nevertheless, respect of individuals often will require recognition of and appropriate response to individual differences. Critics are quite right to reject an exclusive emphasis on winning or on developing star athletes in organized children's sports. But the other extreme, which denies the importance of recognizing and responding to excellence also goes too far. Rather, the adult who works with children in sports will have to show sensitivity and the ability to weigh competing factors as well as knowledge of athletic techniques. As in many other areas of moral complexity, the trick is to do justice to a variety of often conflicting values, rather than to assign exclusive emphasis to any one, whether it be winning or identity of treatment, at the expense of the other values that also apply.

## A Nation of Spectators

At this point, critics might reply that of course no one wants identical treatment for all children in sports or anywhere else. What is objected to is *overemphasis* on a talented elite and virtual neglect of everyone else. But while the critic's point has force, it is instructive nevertheless to consider the difficulties of oversimplistic emphasis on identical treatment, because knowledge of its weaknesses prevents us in going too far in the pursuit of equality at the expense of respect for individual differences and concern for excellence.

Thus, the line of criticism suggested by Michener that we are a nation of spectators rather than participants needs to be carefully considered. Critics of American sport point out that millions of us spend our weekends glued to the television screen, watching football, baseball, or golf rather than playing a sport ourselves. This is seen as unfortunate, not only because of the ill effects on the health of those who merely sit and watch, but also because they miss out on the other basic benefits of participation. On this view, the true result of the "star system," which begins in Little League and other children's sports, is to drive people from the playing field to the grandstand or the television screen.

Even if we assume that the recent revival in athletic participation, typified by interest in jogging, is more restricted in scope than might at first appear, this criticism of sports in America rests on at least two controversial assumptions. First, it is assumed that watching sports tends to preclude participation; that spectators tend not to play precisely because they are spectators. But is this claim really so obvious?

In fact, it is far from clear that being a fan has a negative effect on participation. Some fans, particularly children, may be motivated to emulate the successful athletes they see at games and in the media. What schoolyard basketball player has not tried to copy the moves of a Dr. J or a James Worthy? Similarly, older persons, particularly in such sports as tennis and golf, often watch top players in order to learn techniques and apply them to their own game. In such cases, watching sports events may promote participation rather than lower it. In essence, while Arnold Palmer certainly is watched, he also is emulated and imitated.

What about the fan who is not a participant? Here we must be careful not to jump to the conclusion that such individuals are not participants *because* they are fans. Perhaps if they weren't sports fans, they still wouldn't be participants. Maybe they enjoy watching skilled performers, but would not be motivated to play themselves even if there were no top athletes to watch. So the simple assumption that emphasis on big-time sports in America reduces mass participation is open to serious question, although we certainly do need to explore more ways of making opportunities to participate more widely available to masses of people.

A second assumption about the relationship between participation in sports and watching sports is open to even more serious question. According to this assumption, participation is vastly superior to watching. In its most extreme form, this assumption characterizes watching sporting events as a passive, slothful activity requiring minimal intellectual and emotional capacities. The stereotype of the beer-drinking, overweight football fan who spends the whole weekend in front of the television watching games expresses the disdain in which "mere" fans sometimes are held.

Even if it is better to participate than watch, it doesn't follow that watching sports lacks redeeming value of its own. After all, we don't sneer at spectators, commonly known as audiences, at the ballet or opera. We don't say that everyone must participate in those activities in order to enjoy them. Spectators of sports, like audiences in other areas, often are called upon to exercise critical judgment and apply standards of excellence.

Consider, for example, a fine double play executed at a crucial point in a pressure-filled baseball game. An observer unacquainted with baseball and its rules might appreciate the grace and fluidity of the players' movements. However, such a spectator could not see such movements as examples of excellence at baseball. To such a spectator, a botched double play might seem indistinguishable from a well-executed one, since the failure of a fielder to touch second base would be unappreciated.

While spectators at sporting events can be passive and indolent, there is nothing in the nature of their activity that need make them such. On the contrary, intelligent appreciation of a game involves use of powers of observation and the application of critical standards of excellence.

But isn't this an overintellectualized account of what it is to be a sports fan? Spectators not only appreciate good performances, they also root for their team to win. Indeed, the atmosphere at important college basketball games often resembles a revival meeting far more than a critical seminar on excellence in sports.

Loyalty to our favorite teams and players and the expression of emotion in support of them surely are a major part of sports. As in other areas of life, we develop special relationships with those we care about. Although some moralists speak as if we should care equally about everyone, our special relationships with friends, family members, and lovers are what give life its special richness and spice. If we were not loyal to those we care about and if we did not have a special interest in their success, life would be far less rich and far less intense or interesting.

Nevertheless, loyalty and emotion should not get out of hand. The behavior of soccer fans in many countries who go on rampages, destroying property and threatening life, cannot and should not be tolerated. Violence among sports fans is increasingly becoming a problem in this country.[15] Even where overt violence is absent, the partisan, overtly hostile character of crowds at many contests threatens to intimidate visiting players and referees alike.

Thus, while the critical perspective toward sports described above is only part of the story, it serves as a moral and intellectual constraint on the kind of emotion generated by provincialism. While we need not be ashamed about caring about our team's fate, when we care so much that we are unable to appreciate good play by opponents, the very point of competition in sports is lost. If competition in sports should be conceived of as a mutual quest for excellence, we should retain enough detachment to appreciate who best meets the challenge. Otherwise, sport is reduced merely to a means for satisfying our own egos rather than constituting an area where spectators and athletes alike can learn and grow by understanding and meeting ever increasing challenges to their athletic and critical skills.

We can conclude, then, that even if avid interest in spectator sports lowers participation, which is debatable, watching sporting events may have value of its own. Sporting audiences, no less than other audiences, are called upon to appreciate excellence and apply critical standards of evaluation. Emotional bonds to favorite teams and players, when constrained by appreciation for good performance, can enrich our existence and motivate us to do our best.

## The Internal Goods of Sports

We have considered the claim that too much emphasis has been placed on the star athlete and too little on participation by the many. While each of us may ultimately have to decide what constitutes too much emphasis, some general principles of evaluation have emerged from our discussion. In particular, while our conclusion that each of us has an equal right to an adequate opportunity to acquire the basic goods of sports does commit us to significant encouragement of mass participation, it does not commit us either to identical treatment of all athletes or blindness to excellence in athletics. On the contrary, it is precisely because excellence can be exhibited in athletics that they fascinate us so much, whether as spectators or fans.

This suggests that our earlier discussion of the basic vs. the scarce benefits of sports sets up too narrow a framework for discussion. It immediately generates tension between an athletic elite, who reap the scarce benefits of fame and fortune, and the many who often do lack adequate opportunity to pursue the basic benefits. But this emphasis on opposition between an elite and the rest of us may obscure the most important part of the story. In philosophy, the questions we ask may determine what answers we end up with. In restricting ourselves only to questions about scarce and basic benefits, we may have cut ourselves off from the relationships that exist *between* outstanding performances by the few and the enjoyment and satisfaction of the many.

Our discussion suggests, then, that our initial division of the goods to be obtained through sport into basic and scarce benefits is too narrow. Both basic and scarce benefits are *external* to sport. That is, each can be conceived of and even obtained apart from sport itself. Goods such as health, fun, fame, and fortune can be understood and enjoyed by those who have no understanding of or relationship to sport.

However, in addition to external goods, there also are goods which are *internal* to sport.[16] Goods are internal to a practice or activity just when they can be understood or enjoyed only through that practice or activity itself. For example, the elegance of a winning combination in chess cannot be understood or enjoyed apart from an understanding of the rules and standards of strategy that characterize the game of chess.

The external/internal distinction is central to our concerns in this chapter. This is because conformity to standards of excellence implicit in various sports creates shared internal goods available to the whole community. Top athletes, then, are not taking something away from others but are contributing to others, just as do artists, singers, and writers. Rather than looking at the emphasis on the athletic elite as somehow depriving others of benefits, it is at least as plausible to think that spectators share the enjoyment of the internal goods created by talented performers. So at the very least, we should not apply a double standard to sports; performers in sports are just as capable of creating internal shared goods, although of a different kind, as are performers in the arts and entertainment.

### Reward, Merit, and Athletic Ability

Even ,allowing for creation of the internal goods, however, the distribution of scarce benefits in athletics, particularly fame and fortune, can be called into moral question. After all, top professional athletes routinely earn hundreds of thousands of dollars each year, while nurses, cancer researchers, teachers, and assembly line workers may not make that much for decades of service. Consider also the attention lavished on top college sports stars relative to that focused on the best students at the same universities. What, if anything, justifies the distribution of scarce benefits in athletics, where a relatively few top performers reap rewards that most of us can only dream about?

While the issue of distributive justice is a large one, one important question of justice is particularly relevant to sports and can be examined in some depth. This issue concerns whether the scarce benefits which accrue to athletes can be deserved, since the natural abilities which determine athletic success are "gifts" which the individual athlete has done nothing to acquire.

In his widely discussed book, *A Theory of Justice,* Harvard philosopher John Rawls suggests, "It seems to be one of the fixed points of our considered judgments that no one deserves his place in the distribution of native endowments, any more than one deserves one's initial starting place in society."[17] The talents we are born with and the environment we are born into are not of our making; we deserve no credit or blame for them. Therefore, it is suggested, we deserve no credit or blame for what we do with what we have fortuitously inherited. Since Dr. J. was born with a better body for basketball than I, this accident of birth cannot be the basis for the claim that he deserves more fame and fortune than I do. For one cannot deserve something on the basis of mere accident or luck.

Sports fans might object that in athletics, natural talent is only a part of what determines success. We are all familiar with the "natural" athlete who never achieves success commensurate with ability due to lack of motivation or intelligence and with the less gifted player who attains peak performance because of overwhelming drive, dedication, courage, and desire. Hours of hard work at practice, coolness under pressure, and intelligence at recognizing opportunities have as much to do with success in sports, and in other fields, as natural ability.

Unfortunately, this response, by itself, will not suffice, since the original objection can be pressed again at a new level. Coolness under pressure, intelligence, dedication, and other success-making characteristics also can be seen as the product of natural gifts which we do not deserve. As Rawls puts it,

> The assertion that a man deserves the superior character that enables him to make the effort to cultivate his abilities is equally problematic; for his character depends in large part upon fortunate family and social circumstances for which he can claim no credit.[18]

Carried to its logical extreme, this argument implies that the idea of personal desert is not a basic element of distributive justice. "It's mine because I deserve it" may function as a justification within a fair pre-existing set of rules, such as those governing a race or golf tournament, but it cannot be used to decide which set of rules or institutions is itself fair. There is no desert, apart from agreed-upon rules, since outcomes are determined by purely fortuitous factors ultimately beyond the control of the participants.

Should we then handicap talented individuals to make up for their personal assets? At its most absurd, this suggestion requires that attractive people be disfigured, intelligent ones be drugged, and strong individuals be weakened so that we all come out even. In sports, we might find

> two identical people playing tennis . . . but neither could ever win. The game would never get beyond 40–40 or perhaps since neither was the least bit better than the other, the very first rally of the match would be interminable, or at least last until both players dropped from exhaustion, presumably at the same time.[19]

Fortunately, few if any thinkers have defended such an absurd alternative. John Rawls has suggested instead that the realization that "desert" is based on a morally arbitrary sociogenetic lottery leads not to the handicap system but to a much more plausible conclusion. According to Rawls, justice represents "an agreement to regard the distribution of natural talents as a common asset and to share in the benefits of this distribution whatever it turns out to be. Those who have been favored by nature, whoever they are, may gain from their good fortune only on terms that improve the situation of those who have lost out."[20]

This intuitive argument is reinforced, Rawls maintains, by a theoretical account of the proper way of reasoning about justice. On Rawls's view, if we are to reason from the perspective of justice, rather than mere self-interest, we must reason *as if* we were ignorant of our own personal characteristics, interests, values, and circumstances, so that we see things from a universal rather than a biased personal perspective. The principles of justice, according to Rawls, are those that would be chosen by impartial reasoners deliberating behind a veil of ignorance. Behind such a veil, the argument goes, we would choose to view natural assets as part of a common pool to be used for the benefit of all. This is because we would be in ignorance of our own natural assets and would want to protect ourselves against turning out to be an untalented person in a strict meritocracy.

On a Rawlsian view, then, inequalities in distribution of the scarce benefits of sports may well be legitimate, but only when the institutions and practices that generate such inequalities, such as professional sports, operate for the long-run benefit of the disadvantaged. Such a view surely is more defensible than either the handicap system or strict Libertarianism, since it neither insists on rigidly imposed identical outcomes nor denies all positive obligations to others.

However, if what Rawls means to say is that individuals should be left free to develop their talents and capacities only if development of the kind of abilities in question ultimately benefits the disadvantaged, surely his proposal is too intrusive on human life to be acceptable. After all, possession of healthy bodily organs are just as much an undeserved benefit of the genetic-environmental lottery as, say, ability to hit curveballs. But do we want to say that healthy individuals may keep their kidneys only if such a practice benefits the worst off? Rather, respect for the individual—viewing each person as an end in himself or herself and not a mere means for social welfare—implies respect for bodily integrity. Individuals may be *entitled* to control of their bodies, even if they have done nothing to deserve a healthy body in the first place. Similarly, individuals arguably are entitled to develop their talents and capacities as they see fit. Otherwise, the person is viewed simply as a means for the betterment of others, not as an autonomous agent with maximum control over his or her life.[21]

A system which views individual abilities as assets to be developed only in order to promote maximal benefit to society is unfair not only to persons conceived of as doers or agents, but also to persons conceived of as responders, critics, or consumers of the performances of others. This is illustrated by the following example.

Imagine a small educational community of teachers and students who are joined by a new instructor. Jones, the new instructor, is a particularly interesting, acute, and stimulating individual. Soon, more and more students are attending his lectures and fewer and fewer are attending those of the other faculty. Other scholarly communities hear of Jones's success and try to induce him to join them. Students at his own institution respond with counteroffers of their own. Moreover, Jones's colleagues adopt many of his methods in an attempt to improve their own teaching, and the overall quality of the institution improves. As a result of all this, Jones ends up with far more fame and fortune, insofar as teachers ever make fortunes, than most of his colleagues.[22]

What leads to inequality of result, with Jones doing better than other teachers, are his own choices, abilities, and talents and the responses of those exposed to them. The point of the example would be the same if we substituted Pelé for Jones and soccer for education. Inequalities may *legitimately* arise as a result of our different responses to the performances of others. Soccer has caught on in the United States while cricket has not, in part because players such as Pelé have captured our imagination in a special way and in part because we find the sport meets more of our needs than other activities.

As a matter of fact, many actual inequalities may improve the situation of the disadvantaged. Unequal rewards for better teachers, for example, may improve the education available to the least educated in our society. But that is not the only—or perhaps even the major—reason why they are not unjust. Rather, inequalities are presumably just when they arise through persons interacting freely as agents and consumers. Those who benefit most may have proportionally heavier responsibilities than the rest of us to contribute to the support of the safety net. It does not follow, however, that such inequalities are legitimate only because they benefit those on the bottom. Rather, they are legitimate in part because they arise from free expression of our nature as persons. A system through which perceived merit is rewarded reflects our free collective evaluation of what individuals do with their original assets, assets which they may not deserve but to which they are entitled.

Rawls himself might not dispute such a point, although his view of natural abilities as social assets suggests, perhaps needlessly, the conclusion that the talented person should be regarded as a means for social improvement. Rawls might not mean, however, that individual talents and abilities really are the property of the group such that maximal benefit to the group's worst-off members determines which talents and abilities are to be developed. Rather, Rawls's point simply may be that those who do reap rewards from their talents and abilities have obligations to the worse off, since they themselves, if behind the veil of ignorance, would have voted to protect themselves against the possibility of lacking qualities which others value.

In considering this point, we might ask whether we would want to protect ourselves not only against bad luck in the natural lottery but also against winding up with talents we are not allowed to develop or preferences we are not allowed to express because the least well off do not thereby gain. If so, Rawls's theory implies that persons are entitled to their talents and to assign what value they wish to their talents through the market as long as those who are successful meet their social obligations by supporting the safety net of positive rights.

### An Alternate Defense of Desert

So far, the Rawlsian critique of desert has been criticized on the grounds that it disrespects persons to view their assets and characters as part of a common pool to be developed and rewarded only for the benefit of others. A second line of criticism is suggested by George Sher in his article, "Effort, Ability and Personal Desert."[23]

Sher points out that even if people don't always exert equal effort, it doesn't follow they couldn't have exerted more effort than they did. Perhaps you tried harder than I did, not because I couldn't have tried harder, but because winning the race didn't mean as much to me as it did to you. If Sher is correct here, Rawls may be wrong in assuming that people differ in their capacity to exert effort due to the natural lottery. And if people don't differ in that capacity, it might provide a suitable basis for making distinctions in personal desert. You deserved to win because, while we each had the capacity to try equally hard, you tried harder than I did.

However, even if the capacity to exert effort does differ among individuals, Sher goes on to argue that equitable judgments about desert are still defensible. Even if you have the capacity to try harder, I may have the endurance to train for longer periods or the intelligence to use my training periods more efficiently than you do. While it may be harder for me to attain a level of performance better than yours, it may not be unreasonably difficult for me to do so. Baseball players, such as Pete Rose, who seem to make more of their natural gifts than other perhaps more talented athletes, rightly arouse the admiration of sports fans for getting the most out of what they were given.

Sher's argument suggests that judgments of merit are not inequitable, despite the natural lottery, so long as it is not unreasonable to expect individuals to use whatever combination of abilities they have in a way that allows them to be competitive with others. Moreover, it is important to remember that athletics is far from the only game in town. Someone who lacks the ability to do well in sports may have abilities which can be valued in many other important contexts. This is not to deny that certain barriers to achievement, such as poverty or racial discrimination, are inequitable and unjust. However, it does at least call into question the claim that the natural lottery by itself renders judgments of individual merit based on talent or motivation inherently arbitrary and unjust. Thus, while Sher's argument surely deserves far more attention than can be paid to it here, it, along with considerations of respect for persons advanced earlier, suggests that the lottery argument itself hardly is unproblematic.[24]

### Inequality in Sports

Our discussion suggests that inequality of result, in sports or elsewhere, should not be equated *a priori* with inequity or injustice. Indeed, if the unequal distribution of the scarce benefits arises because athletes create internal goods of sport which we as consumers and critics seek to share, what is there to complain about, so long as the successful carry out their obligations to the less fortunate? For example, the more successful might be required by the welfare state to pay proportionally heavy taxes. Or within private institutions, they might contribute to the less successful, perhaps on the model of the major leagues where revenue from All Star games benefits players who are no longer active.

This does not imply that any inequality of outcome, however great, is acceptable as long as the safety net is in place. Arguably, concern for democracy may prompt us to regulate huge concentrations of wealth so as to keep undue wielding of influence by the rich out of politics. Huge disparities in wealth also may contribute to maintenance of a rigid class structure, which, besides being dangerous to democracy, also undermines respect for those on the bottom. Whether or not such conjectures are true, they go beyond what has been argued here. Our conclusion is more modest. Inequality of outcome, in athletics and elsewhere, can sometimes be justified by the very value of respect for persons that gives equality its force in the first place.

In Chapter Two, we developed a model of competition in sports as a mutual quest for excellence. This model was *normative* in that it prescribed what competition in athletics *ought* to be. Although actual competition does not always fit the model, the model provides a basis for moral criticism of those forms of competition which do not fit. Implicit in the model is the presupposition that competitors strive for excellence.

Some forms of participation in sport will not fall under the competitive model. As we have seen, there is danger in making children's sports too competitive. Excessive or too early emphasis on excellence may only discourage beginners or those who want to play in a relaxed form of athletics. Be that as it may, what distinguishes sports from mere exercise are the constitutive rules and internal standards of excellence which distinguish legitimate from illegitimate moves, on the one hand, and excellent from poor ones on the other. Even those who claim to play noncompetitively generally are trying to conform to the rules and make good plays as well as appreciate excellence shown by others.

Thus, it seems that sports policy in America should have two goals. On the one hand, our discussion suggests that a decent society must provide adequate opportunities for healthy exercise for all its citizens. Those societies that can afford it should provide adequate space for play in the form of parks and athletic fields, as well as introduce children to carry-over sports in physical education programs. However, Libertarian concerns set limits on what the rest of us have an obligation to provide. Therefore, provision of more extensive goods or opportunities should be left either to the initiative of private citizens or local communities.

On the other hand, we also have seen that in addition to the basic goods and the scarce goods of sports, there are also internal goods which can be enjoyed not just by individual participants in athletics but by the whole community. Our ability to appreciate and respond to superior performance enriches our lives. Thus, our legitimate concern with greater participation by the many should not lead us to ignore the excellence and achievement of the talented few. The fine athletes who demonstrate excellence in sports, whether in the major leagues or in Little League, adhere to standards at which all competitors aim and which we all can appreciate. Our legitimate concern with equality, then, should not lead us to equate equity and justice with identical results. Inequality of result need not always be illegitimate. Rather, when it reflects our autonomy by arising from our choices and actions, it can conform to the highest standards of justice and equity in human life.

## NOTES

[1] James Michener, *Sports in America* (New York: Random House, 1976), p. 17.

[2] Ibid., pp. 171-172.

[3] For example, see Jerry Kirschenbaum and Robert Sullivan, "Hold On There, America," *Sports Illustrated*, Feb. 7, 1983, p. 63.

[4] Eldon E. Snyder and Elmer A. Spreitzer, *Social Aspects of Sport* (Englewood Cliffs, N.J.: Prentice-Hall, 1983), p. 162.

[5] Ronald Dworkin, *Taking Rights Seriously* (Cambridge: Harvard University Press, 1977), p. xi.

[6] Jane English, "Sex Equality In Sports," *Philosophy & Public Affairs*, Vol. 7, No. 3, 1978, p. 270.

[7]Of course, everyone can be known to everyone else, or can earn the equivalent of $1,000,000 each year. But in one important sense, being famous entails being better known than most people, and possessing a fortune entails being far richer than most people.

[8]English, "Sex Equality in Sports," p. 270.

[9]For a general discussion of rights and their justification, see Norman E. Bowie and Robert L. Simon, *The Individual and the Political Order* (Englewood Cliffs, N.J.: Prentice Hall, 1977), Chapter 3.

[10]Robert Nozick, *Anarchy, State and Utopia* (New York: Basic Books, 1974), p. 238.

[11]Ibid., p. 163.

[12]However, it *may* not even show that, since individuals could voluntarily adopt legislation calling for transfers to maintain the pattern.

[13]This point is made in Henry Shue, *Basic Rights* (Princeton: Princeton University Press, 1982), pp. 35-40. I am heavily indebted to Shue's discussion on this point.

[14]Kirchenbaum and Sullivan, "Hold on There, America," p. 73.

[15]See Bill Gilbert and Lisa Tyman, "Violence: Out of Hand in the Stands," *Sports Illustrated*, Jan 31, 1983, pp. 62-74 and Michener, *Sports in America*, Chapter XIII.

[16]The notion of goods internal to a practice is developed by Alasdair MacIntyre in his book *After Virtue* (Notre Dame, Indiana: University of Notre Dame Press, 1981), especially pp. 175-178. The discussion in the text relies on MacIntyre's, although is not fully committed in his account of the internal/external distinction.

[17]John Rawls, *A Theory of Justice* (Cambridge, Mass: Harvard University Press, 1971), p. 104.

[18]Ibid., p.. 104.

[19]John Wilson, *Equality* (New York: Harcourt, Brace and World, 1966), pp. 73-74.

[20]Rawls, *A Theory of Justice*, p. 101.

[21]A similar objection has been made by Nozick, *Anarchy, State and Utopia*, pp. 206ff. A Rawlsian might protest that our bodily integrity is protected within the Rawlsian system. The parties to Rawls's original position would view bodily integrity as a primary good—something it is reasonable to view as a means to any other goods whatsoever—and so accord it special protection. But this response is itself open to criticism, for bodily integrity probably is not a primary good since a healthy individual can do well with just one kidney. Moreover, talents and capacities are so central to personal identity that if anything, they have *more* of a claim to special protection than does bodily integrity.

[22]I have used this example in my essay, "The Liberal Ideal of Equal Opportunity and Its Egalitarian Critics," in Masako N. Darrough and Robert H. Blank, eds., *Biological Differences and Social Equality* (Westport, Conn.: Greenwood Press, 1983) pp. 93-94.

[23]George Sher, "Effort, Ability and Personal Desert," *Philosophy & Public Affairs*, Vol. 8, No. 4, 1949, pp. 361-76. Although I rely on suggestions derived from Sher's argument, the argument itself is far more complex and subtle than can be indicated here. For example, Sher does not maintain that all judgments of desert need occur in competitive contexts but suggests that certain responses to behavior may be deserved in being appropriate or fitting. Presumably, public praise for a heroic act may simply be an appropriate or fitting response. It is not as if the recipient did better than others in a "heroism contest."

[24]Of course, Sher's position is not free from objection either. Thus, it might be objected that it is inequitable to expect those with lesser talent to make a greater effort or use their resources more efficiently than others. For a response, see Sher, pp. 372-73.

# CHAPTER SIX
# SEX EQUALITY
# IN SPORTS

In all cases, excepting those of the bear and the leopard, the female is less spirited than the male . . . more shrinking, more difficult to rouse to action, and requires a smaller quantity of nutriment . . . the fact is, the nature of man is the most rounded off and complete. . . . [1]

Aristotle

Games and recreation of all types for girls, by all means, which develop charm and social health, but athletic competition in basketball, track and field sports, and baseball? No![2]

Frederick R. Rodgers in 1929

The quotations that open this chapter express attitudes that have probably been dominant in most periods of Western civilization. The belief that women were naturally sedentary was reinforced by the customs of Aristotle's culture, which kept women largely confined to the home. Not only were women forbidden to compete in the Olympics in ancient Greece, but legend has it that any woman found in the immediate area of the competition would be thrown off the nearest cliff.

These attitudes sometimes have been challenged. However, the challengers sometimes shared more with proponents of the dominant outlook than they might have acknowledged, even to themselves. For example, a Women's Division of the National Amateur Athletic Federation was formed in 1923 to stress "sports opportunities for all girls, protection from exploitation, enjoyment of sports, female leadership (and) medical examinations."[3]

In fact, the purpose of this "creed," as it was sometimes called, was to promote greater participation in sport for all women, rather than to promote intense competition for top female athletes. "Soon female competitive athletics began to decrease. . . . In place of competition, play days and sports days were organized. This philosophy of athletics for women and girls continued into the early 1960s."[4]

As a result, those women and girls who did really want to participate in competition all too often were made to feel strange or unfeminine. Former tennis star Althea Gibson describes what it was like to be a female athlete in high school in the south in the 1940s.

> The problem I had in Wilmington was the girls in school. . . . 'Look at her throwin that ball just like a man,' they would say, and they looked at me just like I was a freak. . . . I felt as though they ought to see that I didn't do the things they did because I didn't know how to and that I showed off on the football field . . . to show there was something I was good at.[5]

While the attitudes that troubled Gibson hardly have been eliminated, the once dominant, inegalitarian attitude toward women in sports has been facing its greatest challenge in recent years. The growth of women's participation in sports and the intensity and quality of women's performances in the 1970s and early 1980s surely is unprecedented. For example, in 1970–1971, 3.7 million boys and only 300,000 girls participated in interscholastic athletics. By 1978–1979, while 4.2 million boys were participating, 2 million girls were participants in interscholastic athletics. A similar increase in the participation of women in intercollegiate sports took place during the same period.[6]

## SORTING OUT THE ISSUES

### Title IX

The changes described above were not easily achieved. *Sports Illustrated*, in a 1973 article, reported widespread indifference, even among educators, to women's athletics, and many still feel that schools and colleges are not doing nearly enough to implement sex equality in their athletic programs.[7] There is little doubt that prior to the recent increase in interest in women's athletics and broader feminist concerns about sex equality, women's sports were separate and unequal.[8] Only a tiny fraction of athletic budgets were devoted to the needs of women students, who were excluded from participation in most varsity and intramural programs.

Such inequalities were defended on the ground that relevant differences between men and women justified the differences in treatment. Women were held too be less interested in participating then men, or less aggressive and hence in less need of the outlet of athletic competition.

While, as we will see, sex differences may be relevant to the form sex equality takes in sport, they hardly justify the exclusion of women from sport or the relegation of women's sports to second class status. First, the recent rise of participation in women's sports is the most convincing refutation of the claim that women have relatively little interest in taking part. Second, the claim that women have less need then men to discharge aggression through sport, even if it were true, is irrelevant to the right to participate and compete. After all, males who have less need to discharge aggression than other males are not excluded from participation. In any case, sport is not only fun but of broad human interest because it is a framework for the pursuit by persons for excellence in meeting challenges to the skillful use of the body, and as such it should be open to all persons who seek to pursue excellence in such a way. The ethic of athletic competition developed in Chapter Two implies that the quest for excellence is a central element of sport. Whether or not sport fulfills other social functions, such as allowing for discharge of aggression, its value does not lie primarily in such alleged consequences. As persons, women are entitled to the same respect and concern as men in seeking excellence through the challenge of athletic contest.

What are the requirements of sex equality in athletic programs at the intercollegiate and interscholastic levels? Does sex equality simply require nondiscrimination? Should coaches simply pick the best players, regardless of sex? Does sex equality require separate teams for each sex in every sport, or only those where women are physiologically disadvantaged with respect to men? Does sex equality require introduction of new sports, such as extremely long distance races, in which women may have the physiological advantage?

It will be useful to begin our consideration of these and related issues by considering the most important federal legislation which addresses sex equality in sports. Title IX of the Education Amendments of 1972 prohibits sex discrimination in federally assisted education programs.[9]

The section of Title IX that deals with athletics maintains that

> no person shall, on the basis of sex, be excluded from participation in, be denied the benefits of, be treated differently from another person or otherwise be discriminated against in any interscholastic, intercollegiate, club or intramural athletic program offered by a recipient. (Section 86:41a)

One plausible interpretation of the above requires that athletic programs not make any distinctions on the basis of sex. As long as no discrimination takes place, men and women have been treated by the same standards and so have no grounds to complain of discrimination. On this view, sex equality in sport requires that we pay no attention to the sex of participants.

The problem with this, of course, is that if it were applied, there would be very few women competing in interscholastic or intercollegiate varsity contests in such sports as basketball, soccer, lacrosse, track and field, tennis, and golf. Although many women athletes in such sports have more ability than most men, it does appear that males have important physiological advantages, for example in upper body strength, that make a crucial difference at top levels of competition.

To avoid the virtual exclusion of women from varsity competition in many sports, particularly so-called contact sports, Title IX departs from simple nondiscrimination by allowing (though not requiring) institutions to sponsor separate teams for men and women. Title IX does not require that each sport be sexually segregated but does stipulate that, through an appropriate combination of mixed and single sex teams, opportunities for men and women be equivalent. Similar provisions apply to club and intramural sports as well.

As described above, Title IX seems to represent a combination of two not easily reconcilable approaches to sex equality. According to the first, sex equality is equated with blindness to sex. Thus a coeducational college that pays no attention to the sex of its applicants in deciding whom to admit has adopted the first approach. A second approach to sex equality is to acknowledge or assign weight to the sex of individuals in order to insure that members of each sex get equivalent benefits. For example, a medical clinic which made sure its staff included some physicians who specialize in treatment of special medical problems which affect men and some who specialize in treatment of special medical problems which affect women would have adopted the second approach.

The two approaches are at best not easily reconciled and at worst are just plain inconsistent because the first requires that we assign no significance to sex while the second requires that we do. Title IX combines elements of each. Separate sports programs for each sex requires viewing sex as a relevant basis for making distinctions but the requirement that no one be treated differently from anyone else on grounds of sex, stipulated in the passage quoted earlier, seems to require that sex not be used for making distinctions.

Perhaps a policy which combines these two approaches to sex equality is not inconsistent. For example, there might be grounds for applying the first ideal to some sports and different grounds for applying the second to other sports. However, before turning to attempts to provide a synthesis of the two ideals in sport, it will be well to examine the pros and cons of each as a general ideal of sex equality. It is only after such an examination that we can tell if each ideal is defensible or indefensible on its own. It is to such a task that we now turn.

**Ideals of Sex Equality**

Like virtue, honesty, and truth, sex equality has few contemporary opponents, at least in public. Even those who oppose the Equal Rights Amendment, including President Reagan, claim to support equal rights, properly understood, for men and women.

What is not so often noticed is that sex equality is open to diverse interpretations. Just as equal opportunity can be understood in a variety of ways, as requiring either nondiscrimination, or equal chances of success for all, or equal chances of success for those with equal abilities and so on, so too are there diverse and competing conceptions of sex equality. Thus, rhetorical support for sex equality from a wide variety of sources can obscure deep divisions over just what sex equality entails and how it is to be achieved.

To those who identify equality with assimilation, a society has achieved sex equality when, as one writer puts it, no more significance is attached to the sex of persons in our society than is attached to such features as eye color.[10] Sex equality is equated with almost total blindness to sex. In the assimilationist or sex-blind society, one's sex would play no role in the distribution of economic benefits or civil rights and in addition would at most play a minimal role in social relations. This assimilationist ideal of sex equality strongly resembles the integrationist ideal of racial equality. In particular, it implies that "separate but equal" is as unacceptable in the realm of sex equality as it is in the context of race. The implication of this for sport is that separate teams for each sex is a violation of what sex equality ideally requires.

The principal argument for this assimilationist ideal is that it is required by the value of personal autonomy. Although "autonomy" is far from the clearest notion employed by philosophers, it refers to our capacity to choose our actions for ourselves and to determine the course of our own lives. It has to do with self-determination rather than determination by others. Defenders of the assimilationist ideal, such as University of California philosophy professor Richard Wasserstrom, argue that only the assimilationist ideal of sex equality is compatible with respect for the autonomy of women.[11]

This is because assimilation requires the withering away of sex roles. According to Wasserstrom, "sex roles, and all that accompany them, necessarily impose limits—restrictions on what one can do, be or become. As such, they are . . . at least prima facie wrong."[12] In other words, roles set up proper norms of behavior for those who fill them. Deviation from the norm exposes one to criticism from others. The effects of sex roles were seen in a 1975 study which reported that 30 percent of the respondents, selected from the general population, believed that participation in track and field would detract from a female participant's femininity, while only 2 percent thought participation in swimming, a more traditional sport for girls and women, would have the same effect.[13]

Of course, no society can exist without roles of any kind. But, according to proponents of the assimilationist ideal, sex roles are especially objectionable. For whether they arise from biological differences between men and women or whether they arise from socialization and learning or from some complex interaction between heredity and environment, they are unchosen. As Wasserstrom puts it, "involuntarily assumed restraints have been imposed on some of the most central factors concerning the way one will shape and live one's life."[14]

The sex-blind conception of equality favored by the assimilationist does seem particularly appropriate to many significant areas of national life. For example, in the area of basic civil rights and liberties, justice and equity surely are sex blind. Freedom of religion, assembly, or speech are rights of all persons regardless of their sex. Similarly, in employment or distribution of important social benefits, such as health care or unemployment insurance, the making of distinctions by sex seems arbitrary and unfair.

But should sex equality be identified with sexual assimilation across the board? What, for example, are we to say of sexual attraction? If sex equality requires blindness to another's sex, does it follow that persons with relatively fixed sexual attractions, whether for members of the opposite sex or their own sex, are engaged in invidious sex discrimination? This is a consequence of the assimilationist ideal that is particularly hard to swallow. Accordingly, we might do well to consider ideals of sex equality other than assimilationism, for the identification of sex equality with blindness to sex may not always capture our sense of what is just or equitable in this area.

In particular, as we have seen in earlier chapters, equal treatment in the sense of identical treatment is not always a requirement of justice or fairness. Sometimes equality is to be understood as requiring equal respect and concern, which requires us to acknowledge the significance of relevant differences.

A second ideal of sex equality might be called the pluralistic model. As Wasserstrom points out, the pluralistic conception of equality is best illustrated by the tradition of religious toleration in the United States. According to this tradition, religious equality certainly does not require that religious differences be accorded the degree of significance presently accorded to eye color. Implementation of an assimilationist ideal of religious equality would itself be unjust and in violation of individual rights. Rather, a defensible conception of religious equality requires recognition of the significance and value of religious differences but stipulates that no religion be placed in a position of dominance over any other.[15]

Unlike assimilationism, pluralism does not reject the ideal of "separate but equal" out of hand. Thus, it might allow separate but equal athletic programs for men and women. While the pluralist will reject rigid traditional sex roles which place men in a position of dominance over women, the pluralist is open to the suggestion that some sex differences should be recognized and taken account of in public policy.

Can the pluralist respond plausibly to the charge of the assimilationist that any tolerance of sex roles violates personal autonomy by forcing women into the straightjacket of outmoded social expectations? As we will see in the next section, the pluralist is not without plausible response. That is, the pluralist might argue that at least some sex differences are not simply imposed through socialization and do not constitute imposed restraints but would arise through an unrestricted developmental process. On this view, sex differences, while they do not justify the imposition of rigid and confining stereotypes, are a valuable aspect of human nature. What violates autonomy, the pluralist may maintain, is forcing men and women alike into a kind of asexual neutrality with its own rigid set of norms and expectations.

Which of these positions is most defensible? Which has the most acceptable implications for sex equality in sport? We will consider these questions in the next section.

## SEX EQUALITY IN SPORTS

### Sex Differences and Sports

As we have seen, much of the controversy over sex equality in sports concerns whether men's and women's athletic programs are being treated equally in our high schools and colleges. Is the women's program getting its fair share of the budget? Does the women's basketball team get the same kind of publicity as do men's teams of equivalent ability or prestige? Are there equivalent opportunities for men and women to play at the intermural and intramural levels? How are we to tell when opportunities or facilities are "equivalent"?

Such questions take for granted that creation of separate sports programs for men and women is a requirement of sex equality in sport. But we have seen that there are different and competing notions of sex equality. Which of the ideals we have considered, assimilationism or pluralism, is more defensible in the realm of sport?

The problem with sexual assimilation in sport is that sex blindness requires us to ignore relevant sex-related differences in the average levels of ability of men and women. On the average, women are not as big, strong, or fast as men, although there is some evidence that over long distances, females may show as much or more stamina than males. It does seem clear that in the popular "contact" sports, such as football, lacrosse, and basketball, as well as in baseball and even tennis and golf, the greater size and strength of men gives them a significant physiological advantage over women. In short, if competition in sport were conducted on a sex-blind basis, women would be virtually excluded from top flight competition in many of the most challenging and popular sports our society has to offer.

Before we consider possible responses to this argument, we need to be clear about its scope. For one thing, the argument seems to apply to sports played at relatively high levels of skill and intensity. Thus, even if the argument does justify separate teams for men and women at, say, the level of interscholastic and intercollegiate basketball, it does not follow that separate competitions must take place in a less intense recreational league. If competition was not intense in the recreational league and the abilities of the participants did not vary significantly by sex, then coed competition might well be desirable. Moreover, in other sports, where abilities did not vary in a sex-related way, sexually integrated competition should be considered and arguably should be required. Such sports might include car racing, long distance swimming, and possibly gymnastics and high diving.

Accordingly, it is an empirical issue to just which sports the argument from physiological difference applies. But is the argument acceptable even in sports where there are significant physiological differences between the sexes and which are played at a relatively intense competitive level?

We will consider three objections to the physiological defense of pluralism. The first is based on appeal to the assimilationist ideal itself. The second maintains that separate men's and women's programs are unfair to men. The third maintains that separate sports programs provide only the facade of equality, not the reality.

### Should Sports be Sex Blind?

To an advocate of the assimilationist ideal of sex equality, sexual pluralism in sport may seem morally pernicious. This is because such pluralism may only express and reinforce the traditional system of sex roles which restricted women's options and limited their autonomy. However, such a rejoinder seems implausible for a variety of reasons. For one thing, the whole point of even having separate athletic programs for women is to expand the options available to them. Without such acknowledgment of sex differences, women would be virtually excluded from participation at the higher levels of competition in most major sports. Moreover, the opportunities which pluralism opens up for women are frequently in sports such as basketball and lacrosse, which until recently have been regarded primarily as activities for males.[16] A proponent of pluralism in athletics, then, can argue that separate athletic programs for men and women, when justified by significant physiological sex differences, not only increase opportunities for women but help to break down stereotypes about the restricted role of women in sports as well.

A proponent of assimilation might respond that if the ideal of sex blindness was implemented throughout society, it would not matter that few if any women played at the higher levels of competitive sport. This is because in the assimilationist society, in which no more attention was attached to the sex of individuals than we attach to their eye color, the fact that most recognized top athletes were males would itself not be regarded as important. At least it would be regarded as no more important than the widely acknowledged fact that in our own society, virtually no individuals less than 5'10" in height have any real chance to play in the National Basketball Association.

But this point is open to two rather strong objections. The first is that we are not now in the assimilationist society. Isn't it unfair to apply the assimilationist ideal, one which is not generally enforced throughout society, in an area where it would severely disadvantage women to do so? If assimilationism or sex blindness is what ideal justice requires in the area of sex equality, fine. But in implementing the ideal, we need to be conscious of the moral and practical costs of beginning at certain points rather than others. In light of what has been said above, sports hardly seems the place at which to start.

This raises a fundamental philosophical point that ought not to be passed over too quickly. Sometimes philosophers feel they have done their job when they present us with a defensible ideal of justice, equality, liberty, or some other value. They then view the problems of implementation as involving only a practical choice of efficient means for attaining the ideal. But this ignores the question of whether it is morally possible to get to that ideal from where we are now. Attainment of an ideal is morally possible for us if given where we start, we can get to the ideal without doing anything morally impermissible.[17]

For example, suppose a defensible ideal of equal opportunity required that we abolish the family, perhaps because different family environments lead to unequal opportunities. It doesn't follow from that that persons already entangled in the institution of the family can just ignore their duties to other family members. Indeed, if there is no way to get to the ideal without serious violation of duty, that ideal may be morally (although not necessarily practically) unattainable to us. Perhaps we could attain it, but are not morally allowed to.

Whether or not the assimilationist ideal is morally or practically attainable by us is an important question. However, pursuit of it would take us too far afield. What we should note for now, however, is that selective implementation of that ideal in the realm of sports raises serious moral questions of fairness to women. Even if society should be sex blind across the board, it does not follow we should implement that goal in an area where failure to be conscious of sex would seriously disadvantage women athletes, at least when that ideal is not yet applied across the board throughout society.

So far we have been assuming that assimilation is what justice requires in the area of sex equality. The second objection is that assimilationism itself may be neither fair nor equitable. We have seen that the assimilationist feels we must be sex blind because sex roles restrict the autonomy of women. They do this by establishing norms for female behavior. Since violation of these norms leads to social criticism, strong pressures are exerted on females to conform to society's conception of ideal femininity. Such conformist pressures limit the autonomy and freedom of women, and perhaps the autonomy and freedom of men as well.

However, sport itself stands as a counterexample to this thesis. We have seen that recognition of sex differences in sports frees women from traditional restrictions and makes it possible for them to engage in highly competitive athletics in a variety of major, traditionally male sports. In sports, it seems to be assimilationism rather than pluralism that limits options and opportunities for women.

Similarly, if there are other physiological or psychological differences between men and women that are of some significance, equality might well involve their recognition rather than their abolition. Indeed, socializing men and women to ignore sex differences may be just as subversive of autonomy as the conditioning of women into conformity to traditional sex roles. While a conception of sex equality required by justice surely rules out a rigid system of sex roles, it is doubtful if sex equality requires us to forget about one another's sex either.[18]

### Unfair to Males?

The argument so far suggests that the ideal of sex equality as blindness to sex does not provide adequate grounds for rejecting separate men's and women's athletic programs in those sports where physiological differences between the sexes significantly affect performance. Rather, the importance of providing equal opportunity for men and women to participate at high levels of competition in such sports is a reason for abandoning or at least limiting the application of the assimilationist ideal itself.

However, if the reason for having separate programs for men and women in the relevant sports is physiological, why use sex as the basis for eligibility for each program? Consistency would seem to require that different levels of competition be provided for persons with different physiological endowments (or ability levels) regardless of sex. As one writer on the subject, the late Jane English, suggests

> if we have a girl's football team in our high school, is it unfair to prohibit a 120-pound boy who cannot make the boy's team from trying out for the girl's team? . . . Our 120-pound boy is being penalized for the average characteristics of a major social group to which he belongs, rather than being treated on the basis of his individual characteristics.[19]

In reply, it can be argued that women form a major social group, the members of which tend to identify with the success and failures of each other. As English argues, "If women do not attain roughly equal fame and fortune in sports, it leads both men and women to think of women as naturally inferior. Thus, it is not a right of women tennis stars to the scarce benefits, but rather a right of all women to self-respect that justifies their demand for equal press coverage and prize money."[20]

In other words, if equal opportunity in sports were identified with simple nondiscrimination, administered in a sex-blind manner, women as a class would at best have only limited access to an important source of self-respect. Indeed, there would be relatively minimal incentives for women to even take part in many sports since opportunities for competition and recognition, as well as athletic scholarships and coaching careers, would be severely limited. Due to lack of role models and other incentives for participation, women would be denied access not only to self-respect, as Professor English suggested, but to many of the basic benefits of sports as well.

Unfortunately, this suggestion faces some difficulties. For one thing, it is far from clear that the self-respect of women as a group is as closely tied to equal access to the scarce benefits of sports as English suggests. Is it plausible to hold that the self-respect of the typical woman suffers, say, because there is a major professional basketball league for men but not one for women? Equal opportunity throughout society may be a prerequisite for equal self-respect. Equal access to benefits in any particular area may not.[21]

A more fundamental difficulty concerns English's emphasis on groups rather than individuals. Why is equal concern for groups rather than for individuals of concern? In other areas, supporters of women's rights argue that the kind of equality required by justice involves treatment as an individual and not as a member of a group. For example, until recently, insurance companies have paid women lower monthly annuity payments than men on the grounds that the average women lives longer than the average man and so the payoff will be equal for each sex only if each monthly payment is different for individual men and individual women. However, many women objected to this practice on the grounds that it treated women merely as members of a group rather than as individuals. Their complaint was accepted by the courts. But isn't this also the complaint of English's hypothetical 120-pound male football player?

However, proponents of pluralism are not left without a reply. Perhaps the most important is that women as a class, unlike men, have been subjected not only to overt discrimination but to pressure generated by social stereotypes of feminine behavior. These stereotypes have functioned to limit the participation of women in sports. The covert influence of these stereotypes have only recently been brought into systematic challenge in the realm of athletics. As we have seen, earlier movements which aimed at promoting women's athletics focused much more emphasis on participation as a form of play rather than on serious competition. In view of the handicaps these stereotypes may have imposed on women, separate athletic programs for women may be justified as a transitional step towards assimilationism in sport. By providing examples of respected female athletes and by generating opportunities for competition for women, such separatism lays the groundwork for a future era when men and women will be able to compete as equals in sex-blind programs of competitive sport.

But this response, which in effect views women's sports programs as a kind of affirmative action, is not a completely satisfactory justification for separate programs for each sex in the relevant sports. For one thing, if, as seems plausible, there are genuine physiological differences between the sexes which are relevant to performance in major sports, the future goal of assimilationism in those sports may be unattainable. If women are on the average not as tall or strong as men, they will face serious handicaps in competing with men at the top levels of such sports as basketball, lacrosse, football, and volleyball.[22] Thus, the defense of women's sports programs as a kind of affirmative action is incomplete. It does not tell us what would be fair or equitable if sex-blind competition between the sexes proves impossible.

The question of equal treatment for groups vs. individuals also arises in another context. Should women with sufficient skill to compete in the men's program be allowed to do so if they wish, even though men are not allowed to compete in the women's program? Fairness for individuals suggests that each person should be allowed to compete at the level to which his or her skills are most suited. But if we allow "crossing over" of this kind, does unfairness crop up at the level of groups? That is, we have defended separate athletic programs for each sex on the ground that group differences are important, but then we make exceptions to the grouping in the name of treating persons as individuals. The male loses each time; first by having no access to the women's teams and second by being bumped from the men's teams by the exceptional woman who qualifies for them. Is this fair or just? Moreover, the women's programs may be deprived of needed talent if the top women athletes compete in a unisex program.

The practice of "crossing over" sometimes is defended by appeal to the example of weight classes in boxing. Although boxers normally compete against opponents in their own weight class, an exceptional competitor is not prevented from trying to step up a class. Similarly, why should an Ann Myers be prohibited from trying out for the National Basketball Association if she is good enough?

Such an argument is persuasive at the level of children's sports, where any physiological advantage of one sex over the other is minimal. It also is persuasive where there are only inadequate competitive opportunities for one sex or the other (there is at present no woman's professional basketball league comparable to the NBA). Is it as persuasive when there are well-established women's competitions, as in college basketball or professional golf?

Whatever view we take, difficulties face us. If women are denied the right to compete against men, their personal freedom seems unduly restricted. If we posit a top competitive level for the best players in each sport, it is hard to see how a male is treated unfairly if a better female player is selected over him. At most, fairness would require the creation of an all male junior varsity, parallel to the women's program. On the other hand, won't the net effect of such a policy result, not in unfairness to males as is sometimes charged, but in harm to the women's programs themselves? If the best female athletes are encouraged to compete against men at top levels of competition, the net result may be a lack of female stars in the men's league because of the physical advantages enjoyed by the males and lack of female stars in the women's league because the most exciting players will be competing against men. In addition, women's sports may lose prestige since in effect they will have been relegated to junior varsity status.

The most defensible approach probably is some synthesis of pluralism and assimilationism. Separate programs for each sex seem warranted in sports where one or the other sex is physiologically disadvantaged. Surely a sex-blind policy that virtually excluded women from competitive sport would be indefensible. This suggests that sex equality is not necessarily sex blindness and that it sometimes is not only permissible but morally required to recognize and take account of sex differences.

However, there may be individual cases where crossing over should be permitted. There seems to be no *a priori* formula for determining them independent of the contextual factors which might be present in each particular instance. Accordingly, implications for the quality of women's programs and for fairness to males ought to be considered on a case-by-case basis.

So far, it has been suggested that a flexible form of pluralism is a justifiable means for promoting fair opportunity for women in sports. But that suggestion is far more questionable than it might at first appear.

### Unfair to Females?

Does pluralism really work to the advantage of women? A critic might respond that if men really are better in the sports at issue, female sports programs necessarily will be thought of as inferior. Rather than liberate women, they will stigmatize women. As one writer maintains, "The number and prestige of sports in which men are naturally superior help perpetuate an image of general female inferiority which we have a moral reason to undermine."[23] This perception of inferiority, the critic contends, accounts for the generally lower attendance at contests between women's teams and generally lower public recognition of the achievements of top women athletes than of top male athletes.

One might reply that in the absence of separate sports programs for women, females would be virtually excluded from serious competition in major sports. Would that situation be any fairer than that described by the critics?

Moreover, the labeling of women's sports as inferior needs to undergo strict scrutiny. The claim that in the traditional major sports, women's programs are inferior to men's programs at similar levels of competition, e.g. interscholastic and intercollegiate, could mean one or more of the following:

(1) Women's programs receive less financial and coaching support than men's programs.

(2) Contests between women or women's teams are less interesting and exciting than are contests between men or men's teams.

(3) Men's teams will always beat women's teams in a particular sport at roughly the same level of competition.

What are the implications of these different interpretations of the claim that women's sports are inferior for sex equality in sports. If (1) is true, it does not follow that we should abolish women's programs. Rather, if women are to have equal opportunity, they must be given funding and coaching equivalent to that provided to men, as required by Title IX. The issue of equivalent funding will be explored later in this chapter.

Moreover, (3) is likely to be true, given the assumption of the physiological advantage enjoyed by males in many major sports. If (3) was not likely to be true, there would be no need for separate sports programs for women in the first place. However, what are the implications of the truth of (3)?

Many would argue that (3) justifies (2). It is precisely because men's teams are better than women's teams at comparable levels of competition that women's sports are inferior and uninteresting. However, while many individuals may accept such an inference, and unfortunately stay away from women's athletic contests as a result, the inference actually rests on a fatal ambiguity. Simply because the women athletes would lose to the men, it doesn't follow that the women's contest is less exciting or interesting. It would be just as fallacious to reason that because the worst professional basketball teams easily could defeat the best high school basketball teams, a contest between two mediocre professional teams will be more interesting and exciting than a game between two top high school teams.

If what is really of interest in a competitive contest is the challenge each competitor or team poses to the other, and the skill, intensity, and character with which the participants meet the challenge, there is no reason why women's contests should be less exciting or interesting than men's sports. This has long been known in Iowa where girls' high school basketball is a state mania. It is surely accepted by tennis fans as top women stars such as Chris Evert Lloyd get as much attention as their male counterparts. Indeed, in sports such as tennis and golf, and perhaps others as well, one can plausibly argue that the women's game differs from the men in qualitative aspects that make it a better spectator sport. In tennis, the power of the serves of the male players limit the extent of volleying and the use of clever crowd-pleasing strategies which characterize the intelligent use of good ground strokes. Similarly, in golf, women must have superb timing and rhythm to compensate for their lack of strength in comparison to males. But why is the more powerful golfer the more exciting or interesting one? Isn't it just as interesting and exciting to watch the timing and tempo of a top female star such as Sally Little as to watch the force applied by Craig Stadler? Upon reflection, we may find that one who charges women's sports are inferior simply has too narrow a conception of what qualities in sport are worth appreciating. If such a suggestion has force, it is not that women's sports are inferior but rather that more of us need to make the effort to appreciate the diverse qualities that are exhibited in athletic competition.

If women's sports can be as exciting and interesting as men's sports, in part because each can be equally competitive and in part because subtly different qualities are being tested, it is hard to see why pluralism in sports must necessarily stigmatize women. It is just as likely to have the twin effects of increasing appreciation of women's competitive intensity, courage under pressure, and other psychological qualities, which need not differ from those of men, and of qualities other than brute strength, such as tempo and timing, which are equally worth cultivating.

Such considerations may have some appeal even to those feminists who have been suspicious of the notion of "separate but equal" in sports. However, they might go on to suggest that if women's performance in what are now thought of as major sports reveals qualities and abilities somewhat different from those of men, why not emphasize sports which stress those "female" abilities?

The suggestion here is that we redefine our catalog of major sports. The intuitive idea is that equal opportunity not only requires equal funding and recognition of women's sports. In addition, it requires emphasis on sports in which women can be the top athletes—and not merely the top "women athletes." Thus, Betsy Postow, a philosopher at the University of Tennessee who has written on sex equality in sports, recommends that we "increase the number and prestige of sports in which women have a natural statistical superiority to men or at least are not naturally inferior."[24] In a similar vein, Jane English points out that

Perhaps the most extreme example of a sport favoring women's natural skills is the balance beam. Here, small size, flexibility and low center of gravity combine to give women the kind of natural hegemony that men enjoy in football.[25]

In other words, our traditional catalog of major sports has a built-in bias toward athletic activities which favor men. The way to remedy this bias, we are told, is not to introduce separate athletic programs which institutionalize female inferiority, but to revise our catalog of major sports.

As we have seen, the charge that present versions of pluralism in sport institutionalize the inferiority of women is at best vastly overdrawn. However, the suggestion that we should develop and emphasize sports which reward the physiological assets of women, just as we now emphasize those sports which reward the physiological assets of men, does have merit. Properly understood, it does not call for the abolition of women's programs in such sports as basketball, tennis, and baseball, but the addition of other sports in which women have advantages comparable to those of men in the major sports of today.

This suggestion does seem to be supported by considerations of fairness and equity. However, two competing counterconsiderations need to be kept in mind. First, individuals may continue to prefer traditional sports even after they are exposed to new ones. The general public may continue to prefer basketball and football to gymnastics and high diving. This may be as true of the majority of female athletes as of anyone else. To compel individuals to compete in sports or attend athletic contests against their will seems to be a serious violation of individual liberty.[26] It is one thing to recommend that schools introduce students in physical education classes to a wide variety of sports, a reasonable number of which are not biased in the direction of male physiology. It is quite another thing to insist that female athletes compete in such sports even if they would rather play such traditional sports as basketball, lacrosse, tennis, and golf. It is possible, of course, that a broad program of education could change public tastes in this area. However, such a program must appeal to people as autonomous moral agents and allow individuals to decide for themselves what sports they find interesting or worth playing.

Second, we should note that the goal of providing what might be called "female dominant sports" as a balance for traditional male dominant sports hardly is in accord with the assimilationist ideal of sex equality.[27] Rather, the ideal here is to assign equal value to the different qualities of each sex. It looks once again as if sex equality in sports requires application of the pluralist rather than the assimilationist conception. Equitable or just treatment, as we have seen in other chapters, is not necessarily identical treatment. Before we adopt pluralism in sports too quickly, however, it would be well to reassess the main arguments for the assimilationist ideal of sex blindness.

### Does Sex Equality Require Forgetting Sex?

The conception of sex equality as blindness to sex is most plausible in the realm of civil and political rights and in the economic marketplace. Surely, the right to vote or the right to free speech or the right to equal opportunity in the job market should not hinge upon one's sex.[28]

But however plausible the assimilationist ideal of sex equality as blindness to sex may be in the political and economic sphere, it seems highly implausible in the *social* sphere. As we have seen, it implies that there is something morally suspect, in perhaps the same way invidious discrimination is morally suspect, in having a fixed attraction for members of a particular sex, whether it is the opposite sex or one's own. Surely, it is not only permissible but desirable, for example, to take sex into account when choosing a sexual partner or mate. Moreover, while sexual attraction may seem like an isolated exception to the assimilationist model, it may well lead to differences elsewhere. Suppose, as Janet Radcliffe Richards, author of *The Skeptical Feminist*, suggests, that persons find most attractive in members of the opposite sex a set of psychological qualities different from those they find attractive in the same sex.[29] Since members of one sex generally want to be attractive to members of the other sex, they tend to cultivate the features in question. As a result, behavioral differences of various kinds, including dress, manners, and psychology, emerge between the sexes. It is uncertain that these differences can be eliminated without considerable interference with the free choice of individuals.

Many feminists would reply that on the contrary, differences are the result of socialization into sex roles, and it is such socialization or conditioning that violate human freedom and autonomy. It has already been argued that in at least some areas, particularly sports, recognition of sex differences may enhance the freedom and autonomy of women. But what of the objection that failure to exhibit sex blindness limits women's freedom and autonomy?

If feminists are right that sex differences, other than in the reproductive system, are entirely the result of socialization, it is at least plausible to think that sex roles are imposed on people in a nonautonomous fashion.

But it is at best unclear that behavioral and psychological differences between men and women are entirely the result of socialization. Many of the differences among humans are shared with the higher primates, our closest genetic relatives in the animal kingdom. Some studies indicate the existence of behavioral and psychological sex differences even among human infants, who presumably are too young to have been socialized. Moreover, there are no clear examples of sex-blind societies, even though the exact sex roles applied to men and women may vary cross-culturally.

These factors at least suggest that behavioral and psychological sex differences have a biological component. This does not imply either that biology is destiny or that environmental intervention cannot eliminate or reduce the force of innate tendencies.[30] It does suggest, however, that behavioral and psychological sex differences may not be entirely the result of socialization, but may emerge (although probably with less force than in our own society) in the course of normal development. That is, such differences may not be entirely imposed from the outside. This is especially plausible in the case of sexual attraction.

More important, it implies that attempts to educate children to be entirely blind to the significance of sex may be a kind of "reverse socialization." If so, it will inhibit autonomy in the same way that feminists claim pluralistic socialization inhibits it.

We cannot settle the nature/nurture controversy here, even with regard to sex differences. For our purposes, we need only note that it is controversial whether behavioral and psychological sex differences are entirely the result of socialization. If they are not, introduction of the assimilationist ideal may itself require the very kind of conditioning that feminists deplore.

Suppose, however, that there is *no* significant biological component to account for behavioral and psychological sex differences. It doesn't follow that assimilationism is superior to pluralism. Of course, a rigid system of stereotypical sex roles does severely restrict human freedom. But pluralism need not be committed to such a system. Rather, it argues that if men and women tend to exhibit somewhat different forms of behavior and make somewhat different choices over the course of their lives, this is unjust only if this produces a further difference in the *concern* and *respect* shown to men and women.

What justice requires, on this view, is equal concern and respect, not identical outcomes. Thus, if more women than men choose to spend a significant period of time raising children, pluralism requires that such a task be accorded due reward and respect. Or if women exhibit subtly different but equally valuable qualities on the job, these should be accorded the same weight as male qualities. In order words, equality does not require the elimination of sex differences (although it might require the elimination of unfairly restrictive sex roles) but rather the equal recognition and reward of equally valuable differences. This does not mean that pluralism is acceptable across the board. In many areas, including civil rights and economic opportunities, an assimilationist approach is justified. However, our discussion suggests that assimilationism is not the only defensible approach in every context. The assignment of significance to sex is not always an objectionable form of sexism.

We have not been shown, then, that separate programs for men and women in those sports where one group or the other is at a physiological disadvantage are suspect or illegitimate. Unlike the doctrine of "separate but equal" in the context of racial segregation, separate sports programs do not stigmatize one group or the other, are not imposed against the will of either sex and actually enhance the freedom and opportunity of each group. The theme of this section, then, is that sport provides a model of a defensible pluralistic approach to sex equality. In sports at least, and perhaps in other areas as well, sex equality does not require forgetting sex.

## LEGISLATING EQUALITY

What are the implications of the preceding discussion for policy? In particular, what concrete requirements should legislation, such as Title IX, designed to promote sex equality in sports actually require?

### Equal Funding or Equivalent Funding?

One proposal that should be considered is that equality of opportunity requires identical financial support. If, at a given institution, different amounts of money are spent on men's and women's sports, then the requirement of equal opportunity has been violated.

It is easy to understand why many supporters of women's sports might be tempted to view equal expenditures as a proper criterion of equal opportunity. For far too long, women's sports received only an infinitesimal fraction of the budget of many institutional athletic budgets. James Michener, for example, reports that

> ... one day I saw the budget of ... a state institution (a university), supported by tax funds, with a student body divided fifty-fifty between men and women. The athletic department has $3,900,000 to spend, and of this, women received exactly $31,000, a little less than eight tenths of one percent. On the face of it, this was outrageous.[31]

However, one should not jump too quickly from the outrageousness of the policy described by Michener to the conclusion that equal opportunity requires identical funding for men's and women's sports. Consider an example from another area. Suppose half the children in a school want to develop their musical abilities while the other half want to learn to use computers. The school buys enough musical instruments to provide adequate practice time for the first group and sufficient computers to provide adequate instruction for the second group. (This was in a far away country where local communities did not vote on school budgets.) However, because computers cost more than musical instruments, the expenditures for the second group are several times higher than for the first group. Even so, it seems clear that *opportunities* are equal nevertheless. After all, children in each group have the same chance to develop skill in the field of their interest.

Now let's change the example to illustrate a related point. Suppose that among the musical group, two-thirds prefer to play the guitar while one-third prefer to play the piano. It turns out that one piano, which is sufficient to accommodate the second group, costs more than five guitars, which are sufficient to accommodate the first group. If so, more money will be spent on one-third of the children than on two-thirds, but once again it is far from clear that anyone has been denied equal opportunity. On the contrary, both guitar and piano players have an equal chance to develop their skills on their favorite instrument.

This suggests that equal expenditures and equal opportunity are two distinct notions. Indeed, the examples above have clear analogues in the world of sports. An institution may legitimately spend more on the men's athletic program than the women's when equipment for the former costs more than that for the latter. For example, football, which is played predominantly by men, requires more expensive equipment than virtually any varsity sport played by woman.

A second factor that may lead to legitimate differences in expenditure are different rates of participation by men and women. Clearly, if more men than women participate in a program, then even if the same amount is spent on each participant, more will be spent on the men's program than on the women's program.

Accordingly, even if men's and women's athletic programs within the same institution are not funded equally, it does not *follow* that there is an inequity involved. Rather, more investigation is needed to determine whether the difference in funding has an acceptable or an unacceptable explanation.

### The Formula of *Per Capita* Equality

Should we shift from a criterion of equal *overall* expenditures for men and women to one of equal expenditures per participant? Proponents of the latter suggestion acknowledge that differences in the total budget of men's and women's athletic programs often may be legitimate but argue that it is unfair that more be spent on individual men than on individual women. On their view, if State U. spends $300 on the average on each male athlete, it should spend $300 on the average on each female athlete as well.

This suggestion is plausible in certain contexts. Normally, if one is comparing similar sports, one would expect equal per capita expenditures on each athlete. Thus, one would expect that as much is spent on each member of the women's basketball team as on each member of the men's basketball team.

Even here, however, legitimate differences may be recognized. Suppose the men's team has national stature while the women's team plays only a regional schedule. Should a college or university be allowed to make one of the team's a "showcase" for the institution? Does the revenue and publicity which the showcase team brings in justify the differences in expenditure per athlete? Perhaps it does, if the following qualification is also satisfied: That is, the university in question must be making an honest effort to turn a proportional number of women's teams into "showcases" for the school as well. "Effort" is required rather than actual success simply because the women's program may not yet be at the competitive level required.

When one turns from comparisons across similar sports to the athletic program generally, the formula of equal per capita expenditures faces more serious difficulties. Since some men's sports, such as football cost far more to fund than women's sports, more will be spent on the average on each male athlete than on each female simply because of the imbalance created by football (and other relatively expensive predominantly male sports).

One might object that rather than accept the imbalances caused by expensive sports such as football, it is such sports themselves that should be eliminated. However, it does seem unfair to deny a football player the opportunity to participate in his sport just because it is more expensive than providing a field hockey player with the opportunity to play her sport. After all, they are each receiving the same opportunity to play the sport of their choice. If football is too expensive or too violent to support, then perhaps it should be eliminated. But it seems quite another thing to eliminate it just because more is spent *per capita* on football players than other athletes. How does this differ from the case where the school spends more on the piano player than the guitar player in order give each the same chance to play a favorite musical instrument?

Of course, many persons object to "big time" college and university sports because of what they perceive as the corruption of the educational process and distortion of values allegedly involved. Some coaches of women's sports argue that women's athletics should avoid the pathway followed by "big time" men's sports. Why, they ask, should women's sports emulate the male example set by recruiting scandals, over-emphasis on winning and exploitation of academically unqualified athletes? Thus, after the University of Maryland considered altering its scholarship policy to conform to the Title IX requirement that the number of athletic scholarships awarded to women be based on the proportion of women to men participating in intercollegiate athletics, members of the women's coaching staff protested and some have since resigned. According to these coaches, "The practice of athletic scholarships is not consistent with an educational philosophy; the emphasis in such a program shifts from the individual to the desires and pressures of the university."[32]

Should women's sports programs avoid the kind of intense national competition, complete with athletic scholarships, high pressure recruiting and large television revenues that characterize the men's programs? Is Title IX correct in requiring that women's athletics emulate men's athletics? Much here depends on what the proper role of sports in colleges and universities turns out to be. (A discussion of that question would take us too far afield for now, but will be dealt with in the next chapter.)

What we need to do here is keep distinct issues apart. One issue concerns the proper role of sports in colleges and universities. A *separate* issue concerns what counts as sex equality within an actual athletic program already in place at a particular college or university. Thus, we can conclude that *if* big time college and university sports are acceptable in men's athletics, women should not be excluded on grounds of sex from pursuing the rewards such competition can provide.

## EQUIVALENT OPPORTUNITY

Our discussion suggests, then, that neither the formula of equal total expenses nor the formula of equal per capita expenses is a defensible criterion of sex equality in sports. Athletic programs can violate each formula yet still provide *equivalent* opportunities for men and women.

But what makes opportunities equivalent? There is no easy answer to the question of how equivalency is to be understood. Once the shift is made away from quantitative criteria which can be measured in terms of dollars and cents, greater weight inevitably must be placed on qualitative, although not necessarily "subjective," value judgments. A full examination of the issues which arise in measuring equivalency is not possible here, although factors which would be clearly relevant would include available coaching, practice time and facilities and "good faith"efforts to encourage participation by women and to promote major women's sports as well as major men's sports.

Equal *opportunity*, however, must not be confused with equal *result*. It may be frustrating to women athletes that their contests attract fewer spectators and less publicity than men's contests at some particular university. However, the games spectators choose to attend and the attention the media decides to devote to them sometimes are outside the university's control. On the other hand, experience suggests that where a women's sport achieves excellence and secures recognition, it too has a reasonable chance of attracting large fan support and national attention; e.g. the women's basketball programs at Old Dominion and USC.

It has been charged that Title IX creates a zero-sum game where women's athletics can gain only at the expense of men's athletics. If the funds available for support of athletic programs are limited, it seems as if any increase in financial support for women's sports will lead to a decrease in financial support for men's sports. Thus, the University of Colorado dropped six sports, including *women's* swimming and gymnastics in order to meet the requirement that athletic scholarships for men and women be given in proportion to the participation of each sex in the athletic program.[33]

However, it is far from clear that the expansion of women's sports have hurt men's programs generally. Although a zero-sum game may have developed at some institutions, nationally the picture is quite different. "In spite of . . . reports of athletic programs being cut back, an NCAA report found that, since the academic year of 1978–1979, the number of men and women's collegiate sports have actually increased."[34]

Moreover, if men's programs lose advantages that would not have existed if not for the virtual exclusion of women from college athletics, there is no ground for legitimate complaint. The benefits in question were *unjustly* assigned to the men's program to begin with, and so the men's program has no *legitimate* claim to such benefits based on past practice. (However, there may be claims to disproportionate funding based on relevant factors, as we have seen in earlier sections of this chapter.)

What, however, if certain showcase men's sports such as basketball or football bring in enormous revenues? These benefits, which it is claimed often support less glamorous men's and women's sports, cannot be viewed as "stolen" from a fixed budgetary pie. Rather, such revenue producing sports expand the size of the pie for everyone. Thus, critics of Title IX can argue, with some plausibility, that there are legitimate grounds for special treatment of such showcase teams. For example, the university may be justified in disproportionately assigning athletic scholarships and extra coaching staff to its "big time" basketball and football programs.

However, in considering this kind of case, it must be kept in mind that men's football and basketball often not only fail to produce revenue, they frequently operate deep in the red. Thus, in 1976–1977, for example, about "one-half of the colleges with Division I football lost money on that sport, and almost all Division II and III football programs lost money."[35] Apparently, the argument for special treatment based on special revenues may apply to far fewer cases than is often thought.

What about the infrequent cases where men's football and basketball programs do bring in large amounts of television dollars, provide exciting entertainment for large numbers of men and women alike and generate favorable publicity for the university? While the argument for special treatment in such cases is not without merit, it should be accepted only when certain other conditions are satisfied. These conditions are moral requirements designed to insure that legitimate recognition of special status does not block the emergence of woman's sports or deny them the chance to achieve "showcase" status of their own. If we did not accept some moral limitations on the above argument we would in effect be acknowledging that the utility promoted by major sports justifies us in ignoring the claims of every person to equal consideration and equal respect. The end result of such a view is that the individual is viewed simply as a resource for the benefit of others. If we want to respect individuals and their rights, then in the absence of severe emergency, we cannot allow the good consequences of a policy to simply override concern for persons and their entitlements.

What moral limitations might apply to institutions where large revenue producing sports warrant special consideration? While it is difficult to formulate an exhaustive list, perhaps the following can serve as a basis for discussion.

1. The sports in question must be genuine revenue producers and not drains on the athletic budget.
2. The excess revenues they produce, over and above those which cover expenses, must either go into the general university budget for the benefit of the university community, or if they are under the control of the athletic department, must be distributed to men's and women's sports, with special emphasis on improving the quality and visibility of the women's program as a whole.
3. The university must be making reasonable efforts to insure that some women's sports, e.g. basketball or volleyball, have a genuine opportunity to achieve the status of the showcase men's sports.

Problems with equivalency may involve far more than appropriation of funds. What is to count as equivalency in other areas of dispute? For example, suppose the coach of a major university's men's basketball team asserts that far more pressure is on him than on the coach of the women's team: It is his team that appears on television, is the focus of alumni concern and attracts major student support; It is he and not the women's coach who maybe hanged in effigy or even fired if the team has a losing record. Accordingly, he claims it is unjust for the women's coach to be paid on the same salary scale as his own. Or what of the claim of some male athletes that many women do not practice as hard or devote themselves to sports with dedication equal to that of the men?

Of course, where such claims are not true, there is no problem. It would be hard to maintain that the women on the professional golf or tennis circuits are less dedicated than their male counterparts. On the other hand, it may be true that in a new athletic program for women, some of the athletes may not have the same dedication to sports as more experienced male athletes. Similarly, coaches in such programs may be under less immediate pressures to win than their counterparts in more established male programs. On the other hand, such coaches may have special problems of their own, including those of motivating players and of working with less skilled athletes without the support of a trained staff of assistants and scouts. How can such programs be expected to develop to the level of the men's programs without at least equivalent support? While the claims of the male coaches and athletes sometimes may be warranted, the tendency to ignore the problems of emerging women's programs and focus only on the (admittedly real) difficulties in high pressure men's sports may well distort the realities of the situation.

In such contexts, there probably will be no set formula for determining when coaches perform equivalent jobs or when players of each sex are receiving equivalent attention or support. The trick is to strike a balance between blind adherence to a frequently unjust *status quo* and too rigid a commitment to inflexible requirements which may give inadequate weight to the special contributions of revenue producing sports. For better or worse, this is far more likely to depend on the sound judgment of men and women of goodwill than on quantitative formulas or rigid principles applied in ignorance of the particular context at hand. Accordingly, while the formula of equivalent support and respect is undoubtedly vague, and surely raises many problems that cannot adequately be dealt with here, it nevertheless seems far more acceptable than the more quantitatively-oriented egalitarian approaches we have considered.

## REVIEW

This chapter has argued for two main conclusions. First, it has been maintained that sex equality is not always to be equated with sex blindness. In particular, the ideal of sex equality as sexual assimilation seems inappropriate to the realm of sports. Second, it has been argued that the general emphasis of Title IX—on equivalent opportunities for each sex in sports—is more appropriate than strict requirements of equal total or equal per capita expenditures, although even Title IX may not give sufficient attention to special contexts where departures from proportionality may be justified. The operative principle should be equal concern and respect for all participants, and this may sometimes justify differences in treatment including differences in expenditures.

The discussion has implications for our views about sex equality generally as well as implications for athletics. In particular, it suggests that equal respect and concern are compatible with recognition of difference. Recognition of difference, conversely, does not necessarily require relations of dominance and subordination. In sports, and perhaps elsewhere as well, sex equality does not require forgetting sex.

## NOTES

[1]Aristotle, *History of Animals*, Book IX, 608b, as translated by D'Arcy Wentworth Thompson in J. A. Smith and W. D. Ross, eds., *The Works of Aristotle* (Oxford: The Clarendon Press, 1910).

[2]Frederick R. Rodgers, "Olympics for Girls," *School and Society*, Vol. 30, 1929, pp. 193-194.

[3]Betty Spears, "Prologue: The Myth," in Carol A. Oglesby, *Women and Sport: From Myth to Reality* (Philadelphia: Lea and Febiger, 1978), p. 12.

[4]*More Hurtles to Clear: Women and Girls in Competitive Athletics*, Clearinghouse Publication No. 63, United States Commission on Civil Rights, 1980, p. 3. For a full account of the development of women's athletics in the United States, see Ellen W. Gerber, et al, *The American Woman in Sport* (Reading, Mass.: Addison-Wesley Publishing Company, Inc., 1974).

[5]Althea Gibson, edited by Ed Fitzgerald, *"I Always Wanted to be Somebody"* (New York: Harper & Row, Perennial Library Edition, 1965), pp. 42-43.

[6]*More Hurdles to Clear*, pp. 13, 22.

[7]"Sport is Unfair to Women," *Sports Illustrated*, May 28, 1973.

[8]For discussion, see "Sport is Unfair to Women," *Sports Illustrated*, May 28, 1973.

[9]More a useful discussion of the background, content and implications of Title IX for women's sports, see *More Hurdles to Clear*.

[10]Richard Wasserstrom, "On Racism and Sexism," from Richard Wasserstrom, ed., *Today's Moral Problems* (New York: Macmillan, 1979), pp. 96-97. An earlier version of this essay appeared in the *UCLA Law Review*, Vol. 24, 1977 under the title of "Racism, Sexism and Preferential Treatment: An Approach to the Topics."

[11]Ibid. p. 104.

[12]Ibid. p. 104.

[13]Eldon E. Snyder and Elmer A. Spreitzer, *Social Aspects of Sport* (Englewood Cliffs, N.J.: Prentice-Hall, 1978), p. 158.

[14]Wasserstrom, *Today's Moral Problems*, p. 104.

[15]Ibid., p. 97.

[16]See the discussion in Snyder and Spreitzer, *Social Aspects of Sport*, pp. 155-161, on the association of certain sports with sexual stereotypes.

[17]I am indebted for this point to Randy Carter's much fuller discussion in his as yet unpublished paper, "Are 'Cosmic Justice' Worlds Morally Possible?"

[18]For a critique of the equation of sex equality to sex blindness in other areas, see Bernard Boxill, "Sexual Blindness," *Social Theory and Practice*, Vol. 6, No. 3, Fall, 1980.

[19]Jane English, "Sex Equality in Sports," *Philosophy & Public Affairs*, Vol. 7, No. 3, 1978, p. 275.

[20]Ibid., p. 273.

[21]This point is made by Raymond A. Belliotti in "Women, Sex and Sports," *Journal of the Philosophy of Sport*, Vol. VI, 1981, pp. 67-72.

[22]A similar point may apply to track and field events as well as swimming, although some writers argue that women possess physiological advantages in long distance competition.

[23]Betsy Postow, "Women and Masculine Sports," *Journal of the Philosophy of Sport*, Vol. VII, 1980, p. 54.

[24]IBid., p. 54.

[25]English, "Sex Equality in Sports," p. 275.

[26]Recall our earlier discussion of liberty in Chapter Five.

[27]This is because sex differences are recognized and assigned weight while assimilation requires blindness towards sex.

[28]Even here, however, there might be exceptions, for example special rights of women to pregnancy leaves, but the issue of special rights for a particular sex will not be pursued here.

[29]Janet Radcliffe Richards, *The Skeptical Feminist* (Boston: Routledge and Kegan Paul: 1980), p. 133.

[30]However, if social and psychological sex differences are "natural," attempts to "socialize" us in the assimilationist mode may be just as objectionable as what feminists now view as attempts to "condition" us to fit what they regard as sexual stereotypes.

[31]James Michener, *Sports in America*, (New York: Random House, 1976), p. 120.

[32]Quoted in George R. La Noue, "Athletics and Equality: How to Comply With Title IX Without Tearing Down the Stadium," *Change*, 1976, reprinted in D. Stanley Eitzen, ed., *Sport In Contemporary Society* (New York: St. Martin's Press, 1979), p. 429.

[33]Synder and Spreitzer, *Social Aspects of Sport*, p. 172.

[34]Ibid., p. 172.

[35]*More Hurdles to Clear*, p. 29.

# CHAPTER SEVEN
# INTERCOLLEGIATE ATHLETICS
*Do they belong on campus?*

**TANK McNAMARA**                    **by Jeff Millar & Bill Hinds**

The 1982 NCAA college basketball championship was a showcase for inter-collegiate athletics. Not only was the game thrilling and well played, it was decided on a last minute jump shot by the University of North Carolina's brilliant freshman star, Michael Jordan. In addition, the two universities competing, Georgetown and the University of North Carolina, have fine academic reputations, and the two coaches, John Thompson of Georgetown and Dean Smith of UNC, were known not only for their knowledge of the game but also for their concern for the academic well-being of their students.

Thus, it may have appeared to many members of the national television audience that intercollegiate athletics had never been in better shape. Unfortunately, if any viewers did form such an impression, further reflection may have dispelled it. In fact, although big-time intercollegiate athletics is enjoying unprecedented popularity, it also is plagued with problems. Many observers consider these problems so serious as to call the institution of intercollegiate athletics into serious moral question.

Thus, only a few months after North Carolina's thrilling victory, another national basketball power, the University of San Francisco, which in the past had produced such great players as Bill Russell and K. C. Jones, announced that it had dropped intercollegiate basketball in order to preserve "its integrity and its reputation." According to USF President, the Rev. John Lo Schiavo, S.J., "There are people for whom under the N.C.A.A. rules the university is responsible, who . . . are determined to break the rules presumably because they are convinced that the university cannot stay within the rules and maintain an effective competitive program."[1]

The particular violations that broke the back of intercollegiate basketball at USF involved payments by alumni to a student athlete and other payments by another alumnus to pay high school tuition for an athlete the university was trying to recruit. However, these violations seem minor compared to what has been going on elsewhere in intercollegiate sports.

In past years, we have seen universities put on NCAA probation for various recruiting violations, including submission of forged transcripts and under-the-table payments by "booster clubs" to players. Those affected include not only academically suspect institutions but such fine universities as U.C.L.A. and U.S.C. Respected figures such as Notre Dame basketball coach Digger Phelps have charged that covert payments to star college athletes, as well as other forms of cheating, are common.

A particularly sad account of abuse of the rules, which unfortunately may not be atypical, is provided by former Clemson University basketball coach Tates Locke in his book, *Caught in the Net*.[2] As Locke describes the situation at Clemson, there was tremendous pressure on him to win. Clemson is a member of the tough Atlantic Coast Conference, which includes such major basketball powers as the University of North Carolina, North Carolina State University, Duke, and the University of Maryland. Many of these schools not only have fine academic reputations but have locations which, at the time Locke arrived at Clemson, made it relatively easy to recruit black athletes from the inner city.

It appeared to Locke that Clemson could not win as long as it played by the NCAA's recruiting rules. While he did not let himself know about many of the recruiting violations involving under-the-table payments to players, which were perpetrated by alumni and boosters, he may have condoned deceptions designed to lure recruits to Clemson. Thus, he reports that the daughter of an assistant coach took college entrance examinations for academically deficient recruits. In order to entice black athletes to Clemson, which was virtually all white, blacks from Columbia, South Carolina, on weekends when black athletic recruits visited the campus, were paid to pretend to be student members of a fictitious black fraternity. A false picture of an extensive social life for blacks was created on what was in truth a lily white campus. The major concern during this period at Clemson seems to have been with building a winning basketball team, not with helping student athletes get a college education.

Unfortunately, these kinds of priorities hardly seem unusual. Thus, the Rev. John Lo Shiavo declares in his announcement of the termination of University of San Francisco's program.

> It is no solace to note that apparently we do not suffer alone. Published reports and proceedings before the N.C.A.A. . . . indicate that other institutions are experiencing similar problems; some of them even worse.
> All of us involved in these problems have to face a fundamental question. How can we contribute to the building of a decent law-abiding society in this country if educational institutions are willing to suffer their principles to be prostituted and involve young people in that prostitution for any purpose and much less for the purpose of winning some games and developing an ill-gotten recognition and income.[3]

However, the moral problems involving intercollegiate sports do not begin or end with violations of the NCAA's rules. We can ask questions about the rules themselves. For example, should colleges be permitted to give athletic scholarships to students who do not need them? What if this results in genuinely needy students who are not athletes receiving inadequate financial support, or even being turned away altogether, in spite of being academically qualified to attend. At an even more fundamental level, we can ask whether intercollegiate sports even belong on campus in the first place. After all, aren't colleges educational institutions rather than minor leagues for professional sports?

This chapter is an examination of the value of intercollegiate athletics. Its central question is what place an athletic program should have on a college campus. In investigating this question, we shall be concerned not only with the role of sports and athletics on the college campus but with the very nature of the university itself.

## THE ROLE OF SPORTS IN THE UNIVERSITY

### All Jocks Off Campus?

Why should a university support an intercollegiate athletic program anyway? After all, many distinguished institutions, including the University of Chicago, Emory University, and California Institute of Technology, have a well-earned reputation for academic excellence and no intercollegiate sports program.[4]

Two questions need to be distinguished here.

1. May universities have an intercollegiate athletics program?
2. Should universities have an intercollegiate athletics program?

The first question asks whether intercollegiate athletic programs are *permissible* while the second asks if they are *desirable*. It may be, for example, that such programs are permissible, because they violate no one's rights, but are undesirable since the money spent on college sports could be better spent elsewhere.

Is there any reason for thinking that college sports are impermissible? Should intercollegiate sports be prohibited? The question here is a broad one, for the heading "intercollegiate sports" includes many kinds of programs, ranging from that of the Division III schools, which do not give athletic scholarships and normally compete only with similar institutions at a regional level, to the Ivy League, right up to the athletic giants such as Notre Dame and U.C.L.A.

Perhaps it is best to begin with an idealized yet influential model of what the university should be. By gradually modifying the model through the introduction of athletics, we can see the benefits and costs which result.

### The University as the Refuge of Scholarship

Why have an institution such as the university at all? What would be lacking in an educational system which devoted the elementary and high school years to imparting basic skills in writing, reading, and mathematics? After high school, students would either seek employment or go for further professional training. Is there any special function that a college education serves which such a system would fail to satisfy?

Traditionally, the role of a liberal arts education, in particular, has been thought to fill a important gap which is ignored by merely professional training and which is not yet approachable by those still mastering basic skills. In particular, liberal arts education, at its best, exposes students to "the best that has been thought and said" in their own and other cultures. By reflecting critically and analytically on the works the best minds have produced throughout human history, students should become better able to acquire a perspective on their own situation, learn to critically analyze difficult problems, and appreciate excellence in the arts, humanities, and sciences.

While similar rhetoric can be found in the catalogs of most colleges and universities, behind the language lies an institution which has been passed down to us from ancient Greece, through the medieval universities of Europe, to the many fine institutions of our day. The rationale for this institution, the university, is to transmit the best of our culture, to subject different viewpoints to critical analysis and to add to the stock of human knowledge through advanced research.

Although today's multiversities perform many functions, distinguished thinkers have argued that the primary purpose of the university is to transmit and add to the sum of human knowledge. They value the university as the repository and refuge for teaching, scholarship, and advanced research. Often they might maintain that the university is in a position of opposition to society, since one of its tasks is to subject currently popular ideas and beliefs to critical scrutiny. This thesis of an adversarial relationship between the university and society as a whole was confirmed for many during the Vietnam War, when major opposition to American involvement was generated on university campuses throughout the nation.

Although the model of the university as a community of scholars and disciples examining ideas and testing hypotheses is hardly descriptive of many of today's universities, let us consider it as a normative ideal of what the university should be. What case can be made for the inclusion of intercollegiate sports in the university, conceived of as a refuge for scholarship?

Clearly, it is not necessary that such a university have a program of intercollegiate competition in sport. Students and teachers may involve themselves in sport at the recreational level through intramurals or informal games, but scholarship can proceed quite well without having athletic departments, football weekends, the NCAA basketball tournament, or baseball games with a crosstown rival.

However, even if intercollegiate athletics are not necessary, they may well be desirable. Let us consider whether they add anything of value to the ideal university as we have so far conceived of it.

### Athletics as a Form of Education

Traditionally, the place of athletics in the university has been defended on educational grounds. After all, if the university is an educational institution, what firmer kind of case can be made for the inclusion of athletics within its doors? However, two kinds of arguments for the educational value of athletics need to be distinguished, since each relies on different premises and hence is open to different kinds of objections. The first goes back to the ancient Greeks, and sees athletics as intrinsically educational. The second, which can be traced as least as far back as the British public schools of the nineteenth century, and which is captured in the famous novel, *Tom Brown's School Days*, stresses the value of sports as a character builder. These different approaches to the educational value of sports are aptly characterized by Yale President A. Barlett Giamatti, who asserts that the Greeks saw physical training and games as a form of knowledge, meant to toughen the body in order to temper the soul, activities pure in themselves, immediate, obedient to the rules so that winning would be sweeter still. The English ideals, on the other hand, aim beyond the field to the battle ground of life, and they emphasize fellowship, sacrifice, a sense that how one plays is an emblem of how one will later behave; they teach that victory is ultimately less important than the common experience of struggling in common.[5]

Let us examine each of these approaches in turn, beginning with the consequentialist emphasis on character building. One argument for this approach might be stated as follows.

1. Participation in athletics contributes to the formation of certain traits of character, such as courage, integrity and coolness under pressure.
2. The formation of these traits is desirable.
3. Therefore, participation in athletics is desirable.

Stated in this way, however, the consequentialist argument is open to a number of objections. For one thing, as we have seen in Chapter Two, while there may well be a high correlation between participation in sport and possession of particular character traits, it is far from clear that participation *causes* the development of these traits. It may well be the other way around. That is, individuals who already are courageous, loyal, and cool under pressure may tend to do well in sports. Rather than developing character by participating in sports, those with certain personal characteristics tend to be successful athletes.

While this objection does raise some questions about the truth of premise (1), it does not conclusively refute the consequentialist approach. The consequentialist can reply that even if we cannot *prove* that sports build character, it is intuitively plausible to think they do so in some cases. Moreover, even if sports do not cause the formation of desirable character traits, they may reinforce their development. Thus, disciplined youngsters involved in an athletic program may have their commitment to hard work reinforced more than it would be by hanging out on the corner. Finally, as we have seen, competition in sports can illustrate values and reinforce them in spectators as well as participants. Michael Jordan's coolness under pressure in the 1982 NCAA Championship game or Mary Decker's determination in her come-from-behind victory in the 1500 kilometer race in the 1983 World Track and Field Championships set examples which many of us may try to emulate, not only in sports, but in any difficult situation.

Accordingly, the consequentialist argument can be reformulated as follows:

1a. Participation in athletics either contributes to the formation of certain character traits, reinforces their development, or illustrates their significance in human life.

2a.     These effects of participation in athletics are desirable.

3a.     Therefore, participation in athletics is desirable.

Critics might attack premise (2a) on the grounds that it is unclear whether the traits participation produces, reinforces, or illustrates really are so great. Perhaps the adulation we heap on star athletes produces swelled heads and even worse. Young stars come to think the world revolves around them and exhibit neither loyalty to teammates, concern for the tradition of their sport, or involvement in larger social issues. However, we needn't follow up this kind of objection now, for surely what the consequentialist means to assert is not simply a descriptive thesis but a normative one about the effects on character in a properly run athletic program.

Perhaps the most serious problem with the argument is that even if we accept (1a) and (2a), construed as assertions about a defensible athletic program, nothing follows about the role of athletics in the university.

Why should the university have the responsibility for character development? If its function is to transmit the best that has been thought and said and support the discovery of new knowledge, it should stick to what it can do best. Athletics may be valuable for the reasons given, but they can be pursued through private clubs, city and village leagues, and other channels outside the university. Moreover, who is to say what kinds of character the university should aim at producing? Thus, it may be the job of those at the university to examine what kind of character is best but it is not their job to impose any such ideal on others.

If this kind of objection has force, what is really at stake is the conception of the university as the refuge of scholarship and research. The British public school (or what we would call a prep school), as typified in *Tom Brown's School Days*, saw its job as promoting the development of national leaders of good character. But that presupposes that the educators in charge had a defensible conception of character which they were entitled to promote in others.

Indeed, if the university *as an institution* should be politically neutral, shouldn't it stay out of moral education? *Institutional neutrality* is both important and defensible. If the university were not politically neutral, it could not provide an institutional framework through which competing ideologies were subjected to rational examination and criticism.[6] Instead, the university would be a participant in the debate, taking sides and favoring one side or the other. Criticism and debate might not be free, since one side would have the weight of its home institution set against it. How, then, can the university support sports as a form of moral education when the doctrine of neutrality forbids it from taking sides on moral/political questions?

Proponents of character building may be tempted to reject the doctrine of institutional neutrality, either on the ground that it cannot be achieved since neutrality is an illusion,[7] or on the grounds that one should not be neutral on serious moral issues.

Rather than debate these points, we would do well to consider whether the doctrine of institutional neutrality, properly understood, does prohibit all forms of moral education. Thus, there arguably is a distinction between values which are and are not required for involvement in critical examination and inquiry into which, on the view we are considering, should be the main activities of the university. Thus, a commitment to procedures of rational discussion, the courage to follow an argument where it leads, and the honesty to recognize a strong criticism of one's own views seem to be presuppositions of participation in inquiry and scholarship. Humility, charity, and personal warmth are not. While there probably is no sharp and fast line to be drawn between the two kinds of values, the distinction between educational and noneducational values, rough as it may be, seems to have a point.

If so, institutional neutrality, properly understood, should apply only to the latter kind of values. Clearly, the university cannot be neutral toward those very values which must be shared if its own mission is to be carried out.

Suppose all this is granted. What does it have to do with the place of sports in the academic curriculum?

A possible answer may be this. If the values which participation in sports promotes (or reinforces or illustrates) are so broad-based as to be presuppositions of almost any cooperative practice—or if, in particular, they resemble the educational values presupposed by scholarship and research—a case can be made for inclusion of intercollegiate sports in our ideal university. Such virtues as courage, dedication, coolness under fire, and commitment to excellence are the very values the consequentialists argue are enhanced by athletics. They are also values that seem to be presupposed by tough-minded critical inquiry, or indeed by any practice that calls for the best within us. If so, a highly organized intercollegiate sports program can be defended along the lines of the consequentialist argument developed in this section. The intensity and commitment which such a program requires, as opposed to intramurals or informal pick-up games, provides a demanding context in which athletes test themselves in what we have called the mutual quest for excellence. This process, even if it does not actually develop the virtues in question, may reinforce them or illustrate them for the whole community.

While this sort of consequentialist argument needs to be developed rigorously and examined critically, it is worth careful consideration. If correct, it suggests that even if one accepts what many would regard as the overly narrow ideal of the university as a refuge for scholarship, and adds to that the doctrine of institutional neutrality, a case can be made for intercollegiate athletics in terms of the human virtues they promote or illustrate.

However, even if the consequentialist emphasis on character and moral education is rejected entirely, a second argument for the inclusion of intercollegiate athletics remains. According to this argument, participation in an intense athletic contest is intrinsically educational, even when its consequences are not considered. Although it is not always easy to distinguish one event from another,[8] and hence not always easy to determine its "intrinsic" nature, let us consider in what ways participation in sport might be educational. For if the educational argument is sound, good sport should have an honored place in the university since it is an integral element of the educational process.

If we apply the model of athletic competition as the mutual quest for excellence, it has several features which make it a desirable supplement to a liberal arts education. First of all, such competition is an end in itself. While participation in sports may bring external rewards, such as fame and fortune, there are internal goods, such as the aesthetic value of skilled performance, which are valuable apart from any extrinsic consequences. Second, athletic competition is a test in which opponents commit their minds and bodies to achieving excellence. In the course of meeting such a test, they can learn and grow by appreciating and overcoming weaknesses. Just as the liberal arts are concerned with appreciation, evaluation, and extension of the best that has been thought and said, athletic competition aims at drawing out the best of each of us in action. In acting for the best in sport, we must use judgment, make decisions which are open to reflective criticism (often known as second-guessing), and exhibit dedication, perseverance, and coolness under fire.

It might be objected that in a good university, the pursuit of excellence is to be found in academics, in the physics lab as well as the history class. What need is there then for an athletics program?

Two sorts of answers are possible here. First is that suggested by philosopher Paul Weiss. Professor Weiss points out that elsewhere in the university, the students are apprentices, who may at best only assist with the advanced research their professors are carrying out. Athletics, along with the performing arts, is virtually the only arena where they can achieve excellence within the university.[9] Second, appreciation of athletics is virtually universal in a way that appreciation of, say, higher mathematics is not, if only because of the special training needed to understand it. Thus, because of the intensity of the competition and its potential for involving the larger university community as spectators and participants, intercollegiate athletics serves as a common medium through which excellence of performance can be widely appreciated.

Our discussion suggests, then, that even if intercollegiate athletics are not, strictly speaking, an essential element of the university, they add a desirable *educational* dimension to it. Of course, this is a highly intellectual account and is not meant to deny that athletics provide fun and relaxation, provide a framework for making friends, and generate a sense of campus community. But critics can reply that intramurals or informal games also provide many of the same benefits. On the view developed here, however, intercollegiate athletics can be thought of as logically parallel in some respects to an academic honors program. They provide special opportunities for testing and growth for the especially talented and dedicated, and special opportunities to appreciate and enjoy excellence for the rest of us. Athletics belong on campus, rather than off campus in alternative institutional frameworks, because they are an *educationally* desirable element of the university community.

### Academic Attitudes and Athletic Success

The defense of intercollegiate athletics presented above applies especially to the kinds of programs that might be found in the Division III schools of the NCAA, including the small liberal arts colleges, as well as the Ivy League. Participants are viewed as students first and athletes second. Financial aid is given only for need, and while athletic ability surely is taken into account in admissions decisions on the grounds that athletes make special contributions to the university community, recruiting is less intense and academic credentials play a greater role than in "big-time" programs. Although many big-time schools such as North Carolina, Notre Dame, and Georgetown, to mention a few, are academically distinguished, the problems of winning at the national level may cause problems in applying the model of intercollegiate athletics developed so far in such a context.

Even at the smaller level, many faculty remain uncomfortable with athletic success. At academically distinguished Swarthmore College of Pennsylvania, football players on the excellent 1982 team became so angered with a review of athletics on campus that they refused to wear the college insignia on their helmets. Apparently upset by the team's 7-0 record, critics claimed that its members were unrepresentative of the student body as a whole, a euphemism for the view that admissions standards had been lowered to recruit a good team. When it turned out that the football players' graduation percentage was 93 percent, compared to 83 percent for the school as a whole, the furor died down, although one faculty member was heard to say on national television that Swarthmore's reputation for academic excellence might be tarnished by its athletic success.[10]

Our discussion suggests, on the contrary, that excellence in athletics should be an object of appreciation and enjoyment for the whole university community. The positive effects of an outstanding basketball program on a university campus are captured in an article by Oregon State English Professor Michael Oriad.

> My colleagues and I recognize the most important functions of the university to be teaching, research and service. . . . But on a Friday or Saturday night from December through March, we cannot conceive of a finer place to be than

in Gill Coliseum watching what the locals have termed the Orange Express. . . . These games are the major social events of our winter months, and our enthusiasm for the team is compounded of many elements. Some of us have had players in class, and usually have favorable reports of the experience. . . .

Most of us never appreciated the art of passing until we saw how O.S.U. executes it. . . . Defense and passing suggest what is often thought of as "white man's basketball"—rigidly patterned plays executed by slow-footed, uninspiring but well-disciplined players. But that is not O.S.U. basketball. The opposing "black basketball". . . involves run and gun virtuoso improvisations. . . . The Beavers, to myself and my friends, blend the best of both worlds.

It is a particular kind of excellence that our basketball team exhibits and that most appeals to us. Ralph Miller speaks the truth when he calls himself not a coach but a teacher, and we teachers in other disciplines appreciate what his pupils have learned to do.[11]

## THE PROBLEMS OF "BIG-TIME" INTERCOLLEGIATE SPORTS

Clearly, the ideal model of intercollegiate athletics developed earlier is at best only partially adhered to even by those schools whose programs most closely approximate it. When we turn to the major intercollegiate athletic programs, the relationship to the ideal may be only minimal. In view of the abuses that have been detected in many of these programs, we need to ask whether big-time college athletics can be justified at all.

### The Corruption of Intercollegiate Sports

The modern large university often bears at best only a family resemblance to the model of the university as the refuge of scholarship. Unlike the small liberal arts college, the huge multiversity includes professional schools, ranging from law and medicine to hotel management and home economics. Its faculty conduct research under contract to outside clients, and its students and teachers are a resource to be tapped by government and industry. Although basic research, teaching, and scholarship are among its primary purposes, it has become what one writer calls a "social service station."[12] Arguably, its job has become just as much to help society get what it wants more efficiently as to subject those wants to critical scrutiny in light of the great thoughts and achievements of human history.

In many of the large universities of our land, sports have become big business. Television revenues and the visibility and support which come with winning basketball and football teams seem to many to undermine the educational ideal of sports.

. . . with just five days notice, the University of Houston shifted the starting time of its homecoming (1982) football game with Arkansas from 7 P.M. to

11:30 A.M. local time for a national television appearance. Traditional campus homecoming activities such as parades, barbecues and alumni meetings, had to be hastily rescheduled, but Houston and Arkansas received $140,000 each from CBS, and the other seven schools in the Southwest Conference divided an additional $340,000 from the appearance.[13]

In order to attract such big dollars a program must be successful. That means it must win at the highest levels of competition. But, critics ask, what must be done to win at such a level? A concern with winning, as we have seen in Chapter 2, is entirely defensible. But an almost exclusive equation of success with victory can have serious consequences in realm of big-time college athletics.

What are the criticisms that are made of such programs? What gets major attention, of course, are abuses such as falsification of grades and under-the-table payments to recruits. But, it can be argued, these abuses are just the tip of the iceberg. What really is at fault, on this view, is the system of intercollegiate sports itself.

If the purpose of participation is not good competition, but winning and making money, won't players come to be viewed as means to that end rather than students to be educated? Indeed, education can be viewed as an obstacle the athletic program must overcome to keep its players eligible. The result may be substantial numbers of players who don't graduate, or players who do graduate, but in name only. Former star Minnesota Viking lineman Alan Page describes a meeting of eight defensive linemen to go over the team's playbook: "We had each spent four years in colleges with decent reputations . . . and I remember that two of us could read the play-book, two others had some trouble with it but managed, and four of my teammates couldn't read it at all. . . . The problems seems to be that these athletes—and there are many more like them, blacks and whites—were never expected to learn to read and write. They floated through up to this point because they were talented athletes."[14]

The highly publicized case of former Creighton University athlete Kevin Ross is an illustration. A highly recruited basketball player, Kevin was something of a disappointment on the court for Creighton. What was worse, however, was that Kevin never learned to read or write or do relatively simple arithmetic. Many of his courses were in such areas as ceramics and theory of basketball. To its credit, Creighton finally recognized Kevin's academic deficiencies and helped him to get the basic fundamentals of a genuine education by sending him to a prep school for elementary school students. It took great courage on Ross's part to go through such an experience, but one still has to ask basic questions. What kind of educational system allows athletes to move on through because of their skills on the playing field in virtual disregard of their educational progress? And for every university which tries to rectify its mistakes, how many just don't care?[15]

Thus, a significant charge brought against major intercollegiate athletics is that it exploits the participating athletes. They ostensibly are offered athletic scholarships in return for the promise of an education, but in too many cases, the athletes are expected to give everything on the field. Little time or interest is left over for academic concerns. Football at a major university, for example, is now virtually a year-round sport. Practice starts in late summer. If the season involves Bowl Games, students may be off campus or involved in heavy practice schedules right through final examinations. The season itself may be followed by a weight lifting program which goes through the winter, which in turn is followed by spring practice. Many athletes don't even expect to graduate in four years but hope to survive on what has been called the "five-year plan."[16]

### The Problems of the Black Athlete

The problems discussed above, particularly the subordination of academic to athletic goals, may apply particularly to the black athlete. Although blacks constitute about 12 percent of the population of the United States, they constitute about 35 percent of college football and basketball players, 45–50 percent of professional football players, and about 65 percent of professional basketball players.[17] Disproportionate representation is even greater at the very top of major sports, where all-star teams in basketball and lists of leading major league batters are dominated by black players.

What explains the disproportional representation of black athletes in such sports as college and professional football and basketball? Theories of innate racial differences have been used to explain the phenomenon. For example, it is sometimes said that black athletes are the offspring of the "fittest" slaves who were able to survive the trip from Africa in the horrible holds of the slave ships. However, writers such as sociologist Harry Edwards have undermined such views with the argument that

> sociological and demographic knowledge indicates that inbreeding between whites and blacks in America has been extensive, not to speak of the influences of inbreeding with various other so-called racial groupings. Therefore, to assert that Afro-Americans are superior athletes due to the genetic makeup of the original slaves would be as naive as the assertion that the determining factor in the demonstrated excellence of white pole vaulters from California over pole vaulters from other states is the physical stamina of whites who settled in California.[18]

Surely, the most plausible explanation is environmental. If blacks perceive many other doors as closed to them because of discrimination, sports may seem the best escape route from poverty and the ghetto. The effects of discrimination may also produce a dearth of role models in the black community; a gap filled by successful black athletes. As a result, success in athletics comes to be more heavily valued in the black than in the white community. Thus, blacks become disproportionately involved in athletics, particularly in sports such as basketball, baseball, and football, which do not involve large expenses for equipment and for which nondiscriminatory facilities are widely available in urban areas.

The following quotations from interviews with black professional baseball players tend to support this environmental hypothesis.

> It has been an avenue for me out of the ghetto. Hadn't I played baseball, I probably would have finished school but I doubt seriously I would be doing exactly what I wanted to do. Blacks just don't get an opportunity to do what they always want to do.
>
> Very definitely. I escaped through sports. For poor blacks there aren't many alternative roads. Sports got me into college and with college I could have alternatives. . . . I've worked hard at baseball to get away from the way of life I led growing up.
>
> Yes. . . . It's helped a lot of blacks. There ain't too many other things you can do. There are other things, but you don't have the finances to do it.[19]

In addition to socialization, racial discrimination within sports also may contribute to disproportionate representation of blacks among the top players. That is, if a black has to be better than a white to get recruited or make the team, as some studies suggest, less skilled black athletes are eliminated from the competition.[20]

If it is true that sports are more frequently viewed as a path of upward mobility in the black community than in the white, we might worry whether black athletes are more vulnerable to athletic exploitation than are white athletes. Since they might tend more often to see sports as necessary to a desirable life, they may be more vulnerable than others to pressures to neglect education in order to achieve athletic expertise.

As a matter of fact, although athletic scholarships may indeed open doors for many underpriviledged athletes, black and white, the odds of achieving a successful career in pro sports are astonishingly small.

> At the present time there are fewer than 900 blacks making their living in the three major professional sports. If we add to that number the black professional athletes from other sports along with black coaches, trainers and minor league baseball players, it is doubtful that it would be increased much beyond 1500. Since there are over 24 million blacks in the United States, this means that professional sport provides opportunities for 1 out of every 18,000.[21]

For those who neglect educational opportunities, athletic talent may be far more likely to lead down a dead-end street than to the pot of gold at the end of the rainbow of professional sports.

### The Case Against Major Intercollegiate Athletics

To review, the criticisms of "big-time" intercollegiate athletics arise from the change of emphasis from athletics as an educationally valuable part of the college experience to athletics as a source of revenue, support, and visibility. Revenue, support, and visibility depend upon winning, which in turn depends upon recruitment of top athletes. The pressure to win can become so intense that coaches and athletes, as well as the university administration, put athletic success ahead of educational achievement. This involves exploitation of players, treating them as a means to success on the playing field, rather than encouraging them to meet their educational needs. At worst, the pressures lead to rule violations, including the forged transcripts and recruiting violations that have too often dominated the sports page of our daily newspapers.

In addition, the kind of disrespect for education characterized above, as well as overt or covert violation of NCAA standards, undermines respect for the university itself. If the very idea of the university is that of an institution dedicated to the search for truth and excellence, isn't that ideal contradicted by contempt for the life of the mind, and even more so by outright cheating. While it is true that the modern university has become a social service station as well as a refuge for scholarship, its primary function still is to formulate and evaluate *standards* of good and bad performance in the sciences, the arts, the humanities, and the professions. How can the university claim a special place in our society if it subverts those standards in its own practices?

Of course, not every school cheats. Many coaches at major intercollegiate sports powers are concerned about their players as persons as well as athletes. The trouble is, however, that too many individuals feel the only way they can keep up with the major powers is by bending proper standards and ideals. As Coach Tates Locke tells us in *Caught in the Net,* it was the pressure of keeping up with other powers in the Atlantic Coast Conference, schools such as the University of North Carolina and Duke, which have national academic reputations, beautiful campuses in attractive locations, established basketball programs, and other recruiting advantages, which created the temptation to cheat.

It may be doubted, then, whether intercollegiate sports should be played at the level of national competition and intensity found in the major football and basketball conferences of our nation. Many would argue that the only reputable intercollegiate athletic programs are those which resemble the Division III or Ivy League levels, where scholarships are given only for need, athletes normally are treated as students, and where competition is regional rather than national in scope. Perhaps this is the only kind of intercollegiate competition that is compatible with respect for the athlete as a person, with respect for the educational value of athletic competition, and with respect for the integrity of the university itself.

## REFORMING INTERCOLLEGIATE ATHLETICS

However, before we accept the conclusion that intercollegiate athletics at the national level are *inherently* unethical, important counterarguments need to be considered. In particular, proponents of major intercollegiate athletics can maintain that provision of entertainment to regional and national audiences and earning of revenue and support for the university, which ultimately benefits educational programs, is not wrong in itself. After all, it can be said with considerable justice that no one would complain if the university's drama company or chorus achieved national recognition and provided a huge television audience with many evenings of enjoyment. If the university is a social service station in other areas, it might be argued, why shouldn't it provide benefits to society, in return for rewards, in athletics as well?

Such a defense attempts to justify major intercollegiate athletic programs in terms of their consequences. These beneficial consequences include regional and even national support for the university, revenue to support its programs and promotion of a sense of community among students, alumni, and friends. In addition, entertainment and excitement are provided, not only for the student body but for a much wider audience. Finally, the players themselves are given the opportunity to compete at a high level of excellence and challenge. Intercollegiate sports, then, benefit the entire community.

This appeal to social benefits is *utilitarian* in form. It appeals to the greatest good for society as a whole. This kind of argument does have force, but it carries the day only if major intercollegiate athletic programs do not involve exploitation, cheating, and sacrifice of the integrity of the university. We have seen that social utility does not normally provide a justification for overriding individual rights. On the contrary, rights function as political trumps restraining us in the pursuit of the general good. Otherwise, the individual would be unduly sacrificed for the good of society as a whole.

Moreover, if defenders of intercollegiate athletics are to appeal to utility, they must consider all the consequences, bad as well as good. Bad consequences, including disrespect for the university, which might be a legitimate reaction to abuses in the athletic program, need to be minimized. So on both utilitarian and rights-related grounds, major intercollegiate athletic programs may operate only within strict ethical constraints. If major university sports programs could be run in a manner consistent with such ethical constraints, they might well be morally defensible.

What we need to consider is whether intercollegiate athletics at the major national level can be tamed. Can educational values and respect for persons be preserved without losing the quality of excellence, the enthusiasm, and the excitement which characterize such national institutions as ACC basketball or Big Ten football?

### Should College Players Be Professionals?

One proposal, defended by Senator Bill Bradley, a former professional basketball player, is that college athletes playing major sports at top intercollegiate programs be professionals.[22] They would be paid to play, but need not be students. While such individuals could attend classes and enroll in degree programs, they would not be required to do so. Rather, they would be paid employees of the university.

This proposal has several advantages. First of all, it would be honest. Under-the-table payments by alumni booster clubs would not be necessary, nor would the fiction that all players are "student athletes" need to be maintained. Coaches could recruit players for athletic ability alone and would not be under pressure to keep student academically eligible regardless of their true academic ability. Second, athletes would not be exploited. Since they would play for pay rather than for an education, they would not be cheated if they never received a degree or developed academic skills. Finally, their pay would be adequate, being set by the market in light of the huge revenues they might bring into the university. Pay scales would not be restricted to the current ceilings on athletic scholarships which reflect tuition and other educational costs. Finally, such athletes could have access to education and could enroll as students, but only if they wished to do so.

However, while such a proposal does have virtues, it may be a case of throwing out the baby with the bathwater. If it were adopted, what we would have are not exciting college sports but just another professional league. While critics might retort that "just another professional league" is exactly what we have now, only with underpaid players, public perceptions are widely different. The enthusiasm of the crowds, the spectacle and the spirit of college sports makes it distinct from the professional game. Students, alumni, and other members of the university community create such enthusiasm because of their ties with and loyalty to the university. It is an open question whether the distinctive character of college sports would survive professionalization.

Another perhaps more serious difficulty remains. Once the university consciously enters professional sports where the *major* goal is profit, doesn't its character change as well? In effect, it becomes a business. If it is really out to make money, won't many of the less attractive features of pro sports infect the college game? Will favorite players be traded once their salary demands become too high? Will basketball schedules expand to the degree where, as is often said of the NBA, players can no longer exert supreme efforts every night due to the need to conserve energy for the next game and the next and the next. If making money becomes the primary goal of major college sports, won't teams more and more often play off campus in the big arenas which attract the largest crowds?

Of course, some of these trends already exist in college sports. But do we want to accelerate them or try to preserve what is distinctive about the college game? If it is the latter, it is in the direction of reform and not professionalization that we should be looking.

## Should Athletic Scholarships be Eliminated?

A proposal that goes in the opposite direction calls for a return to purity in major intercollegiate athletics. On this view, all institutions should be required to conform to rules like those which now apply to Division III and, to some extent, the Ivy League. On this view, there should be no special kind of financial aid for athletes. Prospective athletes presumably would then select institutions on the basis of their educational needs rather than on what they could get financially. Moreover, while admissions offices would be allowed to give special weight to candidate's athletic talents in making decisions, athletes would not be given leeway in admission unless similar leeway were provided for students with special abilities in other areas, such as drama and music. That is, colleges would look for student athletes, not just athletes who might manage to barely hang in as students.

This proposal has considerable merit, and indeed is a summary of the practices of many fine universities which have also had their share of successes on the playing field. While the strict rules it proposes might sometimes be broken—perhaps by alumni booster groups too eager to recruit star high school players—money could be provided for effective enforcement.

However, while this proposal might well be the ideal solution to the problems of major intercollegiate sports, it too has a number of defects. The first is not ethical but practical. Given the huge amounts of money and support which sports can attract to the university, it is not likely that the major athletic powers will cut back on recruiting of top athletes to the extent required.

Of course, this does not show that such universities are *morally* correct. However, a second argument may at least establish that they are not immoral.

According to this argument, athletic scholarships are necessary to attract the kind of top athletic talent that makes for exciting competition. Such competition provides enormous benefits; money and support for the university, enthusiasm and cohesion to the university community, and enjoyment for the region and sometimes the entire nation. These benefits certainly are real, as anyone who has been swept up in the spectacle and spirit of major intercollegiate athletics can testify. The question is, however, whether such benefits can be obtained ethically.

Let us continue the argument then. Athletic scholarships are not immoral, it can be maintained. They simply make education possible for those who contribute to the university in a special way. If the universities' drama or music programs could provide similar benefits, we would find special scholarships in these areas as well. Indeed, we sometimes do. Colleges can and do give scholarships on a basis other than need to attract superior students in different fields. What is wrong, then, in giving scholarships to attract young athletes whose presence benefits the community in so many ways?

As with all utilitarian arguments, which appeal to the greatest benefits for the greatest number, acceptance should depend not only on whether a worthy goal is achieved. We also need to look at the way in which it is sought. If the benefits can be achieved only at the price of exploiting athletes or undermining the integrity of the university, they may be ethically beyond our reach. Although the goals may be worthy, there may be no ethically defensible routes open through which we can reach them.

The remaining question, then, is this. Can reforms be made in the structure of major intercollegiate sports such that their character is preserved, while the rights of athletes and the integrity of the university are preserved?

### Bringing "College" Back Into College Sports

The trick, it would seem, is to make sure athletes are also students who are academically qualified to be in the university, who make satisfactory academic progress, and who graduate with meaningful academic skills. If an effective system of rules mandated such requirements, universities would fulfill their primary educational function and would not be exploiting players. While the importance and contribution of major sports to the university and the larger community would be recognized, and the multiversity could act as a social service station, educational goals would come first. This is the policy that the best of our universities already follow, and it does not preclude success on the playing field as well as in the classroom. What specific reforms might meet such a goal? It will be useful to divide our discussion into two parts, one concerning requirements for entrance to the university and the second concerning requirements for eligibility once students have enrolled.

### Entrance Requirements

It hardly is surprising that those who have advocated reform of major intercollegiate athletics have fought for uniform minimum entrance requirements for entering students. If all students have to meet minimum entrance requirements, we can be sure that all are at least able to do college work. No one would be admitted for his or her athletic prowess if it was clear that he or she had no chance of meeting academic requirements for graduation.

However, several issues arise concerning the nature of the requirements that should be imposed. Should they be the same for all schools or vary according to the nature of each institution? Should they involve minimum course requirements, minimum scores on such standardized tests as the Scholastic Aptitude Test (SAT), or both?

Several reasons seem to count in favor of uniform rules based on standardized tests. Standardized tests can be used to set a minimum level of competence which applies nationally. Courses, even in the same subject, can vary in content and difficulty from school to school and region to region. And while considerations of flexibility would seem to count in favor of allowing each institution to set its own standards, there does seem to be a minimum level of competence below which it may be extremely unlikely that academic success can be achieved at all. After all, nothing stops an individual college from making its own eligibility requirements higher than the minimum. But we still might need protection against schools that might set them artificially low in order to recruit athletes who would not otherwise qualify academically.

In January, 1983, the NCAA, responding to pressures for tougher academic requirements, adopted a highly controversial set of entrance examinations. In addition to requiring a core curriculum, the colleges adopted an additional rule, Proposition 48, according to which only freshmen having a combined score of 700 on the verbal and mathematical sections of the SAT or a score of 15 out of a possible 36 on American College Test (ACT) would be eligible to compete in intercollegiate athletics. Although this is a fairly minimal requirement, it caused heated controversy and led to cries of racial discrimination directed against the NCAA.[23]

The reason for the charges begins with the differences in average scores for blacks and whites on the SAT. According to the College Board, the mean score of all whites taking the Scholastic Aptitude Test in 1981 was 442 on the verbal section and 483 on the mathematical section. For blacks, the comparable figures were 322 and 362.[24]

Arguing against the rule, officials at predominantly black colleges maintain that the majority of their students, athletes or not, would fail to meet the 700 cut-off. Some of these officials argued the rule is racist, since it disproportionately affects blacks and ignores the motivational effects enrollment in black colleges may have on a student's academic performance once he or she actually enrolls. Moreover, many educators doubt the relevance of SAT scores for predicting the performance of black students in college. As Dr. Frederick S. Humphries, President of Tennessee State University argues,

> Test scores do not predict success in college for blacks. Grades are better predictors. . . . Surely, the proposers of a minimum S.A.T. score were aware of the controversy surrounding testing and test scores, the disproportionate impact upon black athletes, and the evidence that standardized tests discriminate against blacks and poor whites.[25]

In addition, the rule may give the more academically select colleges an unfair competitive advantage in athletics. Schools such as U.C.L.A. and Boston College, where the entering average SAT score for freshmen is quite high, would be able to play athletes whose score were significantly lower than the class average. However, schools such as Tennessee State, where the average score for freshmen is very low, might not be able to allow students whose scores were above average for their class to compete.[26] Moreover, this would be true even if Tennessee State did a better job of imparting critical academic skills to its athletes during the freshman year than did most other institutions.

But while a number of these points are not without force, they must not be accepted uncritically either. For one thing, no evidence of racist *motives* on the part of the proponents of Proposition 48 has been demonstrated. The charges of racism stand or fall on two other contentions; that the rule disproportionately affects blacks and the SAT itself is racially discriminatory. Are these claims acceptable?

Clearly, implementation of Proposition 48 would disproportionately affect blacks. But is this enough to make it racially discriminatory? Arguably, a rule's disproportionate impact on a racial group is not by itself sufficient to constitute racial discrimination. If it were, a rule requiring candidates for medical school to be college graduates would be racially discriminatory since a higher percentages of whites than blacks have graduated from college.

To prove racial discrimination, it would seem that at least two further factors are needed; namely, discriminating motive and harm to the group disproportionately affected inflicted in such a way as to violate the integrity or rights of individual members of the group. But it is far from clear that Proposition 48 ultimately does harm blacks, let alone intentionally or in a way that disrespects their integrity or rights as persons.

In particular, as black sociologist Harry Edwards, among others, has argued, the standards set by the role may be too *low*. If, as we have suggested, socioeconomic factors may predispose black youngsters to overemphasize athletics at the expense of acquiring basic academic skills, the setting of a standard may provide an incentive for reversing priorities. As Edwards maintains,

> Rule 48 communicates to young athletes . . . that we expect them to develop academically as well as athletically. . . . Further, were I not to support Rule 48, I would risk communicating to black youth in particular that I, as a nationally known black educator, do not believe they have the capacity to achieve a 700 score on the SAT . . . when they have a significant chance of scoring 460 by a purely random marking of the test. Finally, I support the NCAA's action because I believe that black parents, black educators, and the black community must insist that black children be taught and that they learn whatever subject matter is necessary to excel on diagnostic and all other skills tests.[27]

Professor Edwards position here hardly seems unreasonable. If his view is correct, Rule 48 does show equal respect and concern for the individuals affected.

What about the charges that standardized tests, such as the SAT, are biased against blacks and other ethnic minorities? There is legitimate ground for concern here. In the past, IQ tests were used in unscientific ways to suggest that Jews and other immigrants were not as intelligent as other Americans.[28] Today, concern arises over whether test scores reflect cultural background as much as ability. If whites are more likely than blacks to come from a background where the answers tested for are available, it is not surprising that they score higher. On this view, SAT scores do not predict the chances for success in college equally well for blacks and whites; rather, they reflect the cultural background of each group.

Such claims are highly controversial, and it would take us too far afield to investigate them thoroughly. However, even if the charges do not apply to such allegedly "culture-free" tests as the IQ, they have at least some force when applied to aptitude tests, such as the SAT which purport to measure what students have already learned. On the other hand, the black/white gap is greater on the mathematics test than on the verbal test, even though one would expect the opposite if the charge of cultural bias were correct. Moreover, the whole issue is complicated by consideration of socioeconomic variables. The economically worse off tend to do less well on standardized tests than the more affluent. Since a higher percentage of blacks than whites are relatively poor, class may explain far more of the black/white gap on the SAT than race.

In any case, let us concede the charge of cultural bias, if only for the sake of argument, in order to see what follows. For example, does it follow that an eligibility requirement of a minimum standardized test score should not be applied to blacks and whites alike? Although any position here is highly controversial, there are grounds for doubting whether such a conclusion follows. After all, if the tests examine for skills that it is important for everyone to have in our culture—basic skills in writing and mathematics—blacks no less than whites need to acquire them. Arguably, it is racist to demand less of ethnic minorities than others, especially when they will need basic skills to succeed in the culture as a whole.

Should we conclude that Rule 48 is justified, or even go further and assert, with Harry Edwards, that the minimum requirement it sets is too *low*? Although there is much to be said for such a view, it does leave out one important factor. Higher education in America is extraordinarily diverse. The average test scores of students at schools such as Stanford, Duke, and Michigan are much higher than those at many other institutions. Why prevent students from playing at Tennessee State if their scores are above average for their school while permitting students to play at Duke even if their scores are below average for that particular institution? As several presidents of black universities argue, such a policy may be counterproductive since sports is what induces many students to attend their school in the first place.

Perhaps a better approach to eligibility requirements would be to relativize them to each institution. For example, why not stipulate that freshmen are eligible for intercollegiate athletics only if their scores on the SAT or ACT are in the top two thirds of the entering class in their own institution. Athletes who failed to meet this requirement would, of course, still be able to enroll as students, as is also allowed by Rule 48, but would have the freshman year to adjust academically without the pressures of intercollegiate varsity competition.

Alternately, the NCAA may prohibit all freshmen from participating in intercollegiate varsity athletics. This proposal does have the advantage of providing a year for everyone to adjust to the rigors of college work. In addition, the freshman year could be used to insure that all athletes saw themselves as students first. Freshmen football players, for example, would not have to arrive on campus before classes for preseason practice. Instead, they would arrive with other new students. They would have the opportunity to meet all kinds of people and would not be segregated in special dormitories for athletes. While it may seem unfair to prevent academically well-qualified students from participating, it seems even more unfair to expect athletes to participate in a high pressure varsity program and to do well academically on the college level without providing a period for measured adjustment to the rigorous new demands made upon them in class and on the field alike.

The conclusion that emerges from our discussion is that the use of standardized test scores as eligibility tests for participation by freshmen in intercollegiate sports is justified. However, while Rule 48 may be more defensible than its critics allow, a standard relativized to the academic demands of each particular university is more reasonable than the across-the-board standard established by Rule 48. The best approach, which would make Rule 48 unnecessary, is to prohibit freshmen from participating in major (Division I) intercollegiate varsity programs in the first place.

### Eligibility Requirements

Overall, it is far from clear that participation in athletics adversely affects academic performance.[29] Participation in sports by itself may not be academically harmful, and may even be beneficial. However, it is far from clear that many major college athletic programs are sufficiently concerned for the academic success of their athletes. Thus, one former athlete reports that his university

> recruited top football players regardless of their academic ability, and the athletic department's biggest jobs were to get football players admitted and then to keep them eligible. I remember one citizenship course which all . . . freshmen were required to take. I knew most of the other players

hadn't been going to class or done any studying and I couldn't figure out how they were going to pass. . . . Then, just before midterms, we had a . . . meeting with one of the tutors hired by the athletic department. . . . He told us cryptically that if we copied down what he said we would do all right on the exam. He wasn't joking: when I took the exam I discovered he had given us the answers to the test questions.[30]

While we can hope that such practices are not typical, it is clear that if colleges and universities are to avoid exploiting players by treating them as mere means for gaining money and support through sports, genuine concern needs to be shown for their education. It is not enough for the NCAA to require some minimum average in a course of study as a condition for eligibility. For one thing, no protection is provided for the athlete after he or she uses up athletic eligibility. Second, no rules apply to what is studied. Surely the curriculum of athletes should not consist largely of courses such as Theory of Basketball and Recreation 110.

There are many suggestions concerning how academic requirements for athletes in Division I schools might be made more rigorous. Perhaps most attractive is a three-pronged approach which would require that

1. graduation rates for athletes in each school's intercollegiate program (or in each sport within that program) not vary significantly from the graduation rate for the student body as a whole,
2. tutoring provided for athletes be administered by academic authorities, each as the faculty, rather than the athletic department, and not differ in kind from that available for other students at academic risk,
3. course selection for athletes be entirely in the hands of academic advisors and not the athletic department,
4. participants in intercollegiate athletics be required to take a core of courses stressing development of writing and critical skills, as well as acquaintance with science or mathematics and art.

The last requirement is particularly controversial since it may require more of athletes than some institutions do of other students. On the other hand, if institutions really are promising prospective athletes an education in return for performance on the field, they have a responsibility to insure that a meaningful education is in fact provided.

Regardless of what specific reforms are best, the moral point is clear. The administration and faculties of universities that engage in major intercollegiate sports have a moral obligation to make sure their players are not treated merely as means for attaining victory and the kind of support that goes with it. Only an infinitesimal percentage of such athletes will have successful careers in pro sports. The university can avoid exploitation, then, by seeing that their athletes acquire the educational background to enable them to develop their full potential, appreciate the culture around them, and lead productive lives. While many universities, including some of the major sports powers, may already meet these goals, it is those that do not that contribute to the present blight on intercollegiate athletics.

## CONCLUSIONS

The ideal role for intercollegiate athletics in the university, it has been argued, is educational. At their best, intercollegiate athletics allow for development, reinforcement, and expression of desirable traits of character—the virtues. In addition, they provide a test of mind and body for participants and an example for the rest of the community of men and women trying their best to achieve excellence. At its best, the university is a place where standards of truth and excellence are formulated, defended, and applied in the arts, sciences, and humanities. Competitive sports provide a clear institutional framework in which the concern for achieving excellence through challenge is demonstrated and reinforced. In addition, intercollegiate sports help make a university a community by providing fun and recreation for its members. Intercollegiate athletics, then, can support rather than contradict the basic mission of the university as a refuge for teaching, scholarship, and research.

Of course, the large multiversity of today is more than a refuge for scholarship and research. It provides professional training and certification, is a source of expertise for government and industry and can be the cultural focus for an entire community, region, or state. Athletics can be an important source of revenue and support for such a university. In addition, its teams may provide entertainment for great masses of people, who come to identify with the institution and its goals. In short, intercollegiate sports can promote many socially desirable goals and hence can be defended on utilitarian grounds.

However, pursuit of those goals must not violate ethical constraints. In particular, college athletes should not be exploited and the university should not violate its own ideals. Even if the modern university is not simply a refuge for scholarship, the university is a virtually unique institution in our society. Its primary function still must be to preserve critical standards of inquiry and reflection in the pursuit of truth. No other institution is charged with this task. This task is so vital not only because it is socially useful in a utilitarian sense,[31] but also because without such standards, we could not function well as free autonomous agents. Rather, we would more easily be victimized by ignorance, prejudice, and insularity. Thus, while the university has many functions, it has the special mission of looking at our society, as well as others, and measuring it against the best that has been thought and said in human history. Surely it is indefensible for the very institution charged with keeping standards of truth and excellence before our minds to cheat in order to win ball games or to merely use athletes to achieve fame and fortune, ignoring the educational goals it is supposed to protect.

While trying to raise funds before a state legislature, a midwestern university president is said to have asserted, "We need money to build a university our football team can be proud of." On the contrary, the institutions involved in intercollegiate sports will have much to be proud of only when their major teams are genuinely part of the educational community that comprises the heart of the university.

## NOTES

[1]Rev. John Lo Schiavo, "Trying to Save a University's Priceless Assets," *The New York Times*, August 1, 1982, p. S2. © 1982 by The New York Times Company. Reprinted by permission.

[2]Tates Locke and Bob Ibach, *Caught in the Net* (West Point, New York: Leisure Press, 1982).

[3]Rev. John Lo Schiavo, "Trying to Save a University's Priceless Assets."

[4]This point is made by George H. Sage in his essay, "The Collegiate Dilemma of Sport and Leisure: A Sociological Perspective," in D. Stanley Eitzen, ed., *Sport in Contemporary Society* (New York: St. Martin's Press, 1979), p. 191. Sage's article is a thoughtful critique of the involvement of colleges and universities in big-time sport.

[5]A. Bartlett Giamatti, address to the Association of Yale Alumni, XVI, April 10, 1980, p. 4, reprinted by permission.

[6]The principle that the university as an institution should be politically neutral is criticized by Robert Paul Wolff in his book, *The Ideal of the University* (Boston: Beacon Press, 1969), pp. 69-76. A response to Wolff and a defense of the principle is found in Robert L. Simon, "The Concept of a Politically Neutral University," in Virginia Held, Kai Nielson, and Charles Parsons, *Philosophy & Political Action* (New York: Oxford University Press, 1972), pp. 217-233.

[7]Wolff's remarks on neutrality in *The Ideal of the University*, referred to above, contain arguments for the view that the university *cannot* be politically neutral, no matter how hard it tries.

[8]For example, if Jones pulls the trigger of a revolver, thereby killing Smith, is the killing of Smith a second event caused by the earlier event of Jones pulling the trigger, or is there just one event, namely, Jones killing Smith by gunshot?

[9]Paul Weiss, *Sport: A Philosophic Inquiry* (Carbondale, Illinois: Southern Illinois University Press, 1969), pp. 10-13.

[10]For a discussion of the acute discomfort engendered in the Swarthmore community by the success of its football team, see Frank Brady, "Swarthmore's Shakespearean Cast and Other Tales, *The New York Times*, Nov. 1, 1982, p. C6.

[11]Michael Oriad, "At Oregon State, Basketball is Pleasing, Not Alarming," *The New York Times*, March 8, 1981, p. S2. © 1981 by The New York Times Company. Reprinted by permission.

[12]For an account of different conceptions of the university to which my own discussion is in debt, see Robert Paul Wolff, *The Ideal of the University*.

[13]Neil Amdur, "The Changing Face of Sports: The Television Dollars Foster New Perceptions," *The New York Times*, October 30, 1982, p. 9. © 1982 by The New York Times Company. Reprinted by permission.

[14]Ira Berkow, "College 'Factories' and Their Output," *The New York Times*, Jan. 18, 1983, p. D25. © 1983 by The New York Times Company. Reprinted by permission.

[15]For an account of the Ross case, see Edward Menaker, "Casualty of a Failed System," *The New York Times*, Oct. 3, 1982, p. S11.

[16]Of course, athletes are not the only students who take more than the "normal" four years to graduate. Unfortunately, reliable data on comparative academic performance of athletes and nonathletes is hard to obtain and often inconclusive when available. For a summary of some relevant studies, see Eldon E. Snyder and Elmer A. Spreitzer, *Social Aspects of Sport* (Englewood Cliffs, N.J.: Prentice-Hall, 1983), pp. 133-137.

[17]Ibid., pp. 175-176.

[18]Harry Edwards, *Sociology of Sport* (Homeward, Illinois: The Dorsey Press, 1973), p. 198. See Edwards for thoughtful criticism of genetic explanations of disproportional representation of blacks in many major sports.

[19]Snyder and Spreitzer, *Social Aspects of Sport*, p. 189.

[20]For discussion, see Edwards, *Sociology of Sport*, Chapter 7 and Snyder and Spreitzer, *Social Aspects of Sport*, Chapter 11.

[21]Jay Coakley, *Sport in Society* (St. Louis, Mo.: C.V. Mosby Co., 1978), p. 295, quoted by Snyder and Spreitzer, Ibid., p. 190.

[22]Bill Bradley has expressed his views in various columns and interviews. See for example, *The Lexington Leader*, Lexington, Kentucky, March 31, 1982, Section C, p. 1.

[23]See "Black Colleges Threaten to Leave N.C.A.A. Over Testing," *The New York Times*, Jan. 13, 1983, p. 1.

[24]Edward B. Fiske, "Athletes' Test Scores," *The New York Times*, Jan. 14, 1983, p. A11.

[25]Frederick S. Humphries, "New Academic Standard: Is It Fair? Will It Work?" *The New York Times*, Jan. 16, 1983, p. 2S. © 1983 by The New York Times Company. Reprinted by permission.

[26]This point is made by Humphries, Ibid.

[27]Harry Edwards, "Educating Black Athletes," *The Atlantic Monthly*, August, 1983, pp. 36-37. Copyright © 1983, by The Atlantic Monthly Company, Boston, Mass. Reprinted with permission.

[28]See Stephen Jay Gould, *The Mismeasure of Man* (New York: W.W. Norton & Company, 1981).

[29]See G. H. Hanford, *The Need for and Feasibility of a Study of Intercollegiate Athletics* (Washington, D.C.: American Council of Education, 1974), pp. 131-132.

[30]Dave Meggysey, *Out of Their League* (Palo Alto: Rampart Press, 1971), pp. 43-44.

[31]Without a concern for such standards of truth and excellence, it is plausible to think that society would be less likely to seek criticism and improvement. Error, and consequent disutility, would be frozen in.

# EPILOGUE
## *Sports and human values*

The principal argument running through our discussions is that sports raise a host of significant ethical issues. At their best, sports can constitute a stimulating challenge to our minds and bodies. At its worst, they can be a joyless endeavor where losing is equated with personal failure and winning is just a way to get external reward.

Our discussion suggests that sports provides internal goods of important human significance. Although sports cannot be compared to science, the arts, or the humanities in terms of the cosmic significance of its subject matter, or in the human importance of its achievement, this is not to say it is unimportant or trivial. Through sports, we can face and overcome challenges and develop a concern for excellence. We can engage in activities that we value for themselves, apart from the rewards that accrue to the most successful. Sports can raise the human spirit and provide enjoyment and involvement for millions. Through sports we can develop and express moral virtues and vices, and demonstrate the importance of such values as loyalty, dedication, integrity, and courage.

However, if we are to have good sports rather than bad ones, we need to reflect on the principles that govern our athletic institutions and practices. Whether or not we accept the ethic of athletic competition as the mutual quest for excellence, we need to have some ethical standard in order to distinguish good sports from bad. That standard can be arrived at only through the kind of critical reflection that is characteristic of philosophic inquiry.

If the view of sport developed here is defensible, the goal is worth the effort. We can do worse than conclude with the remarks of Socrates, in Plato's *Republic,* who mentions gymnastics but surely is speaking of sport in a more general sense, when he maintains that

> it seems there are two arts which I would say some god gave to mankind, music and gymnastics, for the service of the high spirited principle and the love of knowledge in them—not for the soul and body incidentally, but for their harmonious adjustment. (Bk. III, 412)

# INDEX